The Anatomy of the Feature Model

A Guide to Lean Requirements Modeling

by

Mike Brennan

All illustrations in this book were generated from Enterprise Architect. Enterprise Architect is a software modeling tool and is a product of Sparx Systems, Inc. **http://www.sparxsystems.com**.

The companion website for this book is **http://stickmanllc.com/anatomy**.

ISBN-13: 978-1470048297

ISBN-10: 1470048299

First Printing April 2012

For Paul, Jeanne, Chip, Kathy, Cindy, Ernie, Jamie, Will, Michael and especially John and Mike H., who inspired me both good and bad.

Special Thanks to Junifer for editing and Timi for the cover art.

Contents

Introduction

The software development process has been called many things including art, science and even a rugby game. But every process, no matter what it is called, is made up of a series of steps that move toward a goal. The problem with software, unlike a rugby game, is that the goal is usually not completely understood until the project is finished. It's a game where the goal of the game is to discover the goal. There have been many methodologies tried but all fail at the same point... at the beginning. You can imagine that if you are not sure what the end goal is, that knowing how to start the game might be a little difficult.

Many have discovered that documenting and coming to a common understanding of what the User wants the system to do is the best place to start. These "wants" are called "features". The acronym INVEST has been used to describe a Feature. The Feature is a piece of software that is "independent, negotiable, valuable, estimateable, small and testable." It is a unit of work that meets a specific customer need and can be built within a short software development cycle. The problem is, how do we document the Feature so that it can be determine if it actually fits the INVEST rule before we embark on a build plan?

This book introduces the Feature Model as the answer. More than a "User Story", less than a "Requirements Specification", the Feature Model minimizes redundant conversations by consolidating the questions and answers about a single software feature into one cohesive software model. Now, the feature can be visualized to see if it really meets the INVEST rule. If it passes the test, then the model is presented to the development team as a request to build. The model itself is designed to be as lean as possible while pulling together just enough information to create the feature.

This book will teach you how to read and navigate a Feature Model. The Feature Model uses standard UML[1] terminology and is designed to do two things. One, it is designed to allow the customer to visualize the feature before any code is written. Two, it is designed to give the programmer answers to the usual questions that must be asked before they can begin writing code. The building of a Feature Model takes only a few hours, so the theory here is that this will save time, money and wasted effort for both the customer and the programmer. This Model will allow the customer to make better decisions about what and when to build. It will also reduce the amount of time a programmer takes to chase down a busy customer to ask a question. And, who doesn't want to save time and money?

What's in the book?

The book is based upon a single example that you may view at **http://Stickmanllc.Com/anatomy**. The example describes a feature called "Outage Summary." The book proceeds step by step to show you how to navigate and read this model. For the most part, the Feature Model is non-technical and anyone can understand the symbols used. But there are hidden details in the model that are primarily for the programmers. These details will be explained along the way.

Where do I start?

The first two chapters of the book discuss problems that arise in human communication that lead to bad requirements. Avoiding these problems takes a targeted approach to getting correct requirements. In summary, theses chapters point out that incorrect requirements cause projects to fail. Requirements are incorrect due to poor communication techniques. Two communication techniques

---

[1] UML: Unified Modeling Language

solve the communication failure. They are "Trust but Verify" and "Formalize to Simplify". The Feature Model targets software requirements using these two techniques. If you are already comfortable with these ideas, then jump over to Chapter 3. Chapter 3 gets right into describing the model and the rest of the book moves step by step thru the model. As there are many parts (or smaller models) to the Feature Model, each of the following chapters explains a single part of the model.

Use the Web Site

The website at **http://stickmanllc.com/anatomy** is a complete working Feature Model. The book is built around this model. So, it will be extremely beneficial to work your way through this model as you read through the book.

Chapter 1: Why this?

The Toughest Job

The toughest part of any software project is getting, capturing and communicating the correct requirements. What a customer says they want is not always what they need. Customers usually speak from their own experience about a possible solution to a problem rather than about the problem they want to solve. It is the analyst's job to listen with the idea of first discovering the problem, verifying the problem with the customer and then presenting a possible software solution. It is said that "80 to 85 percent of software project failures are due to incorrect requirements" (Leffingwell, 2011) (Reinertsen, 2009). When you think about it, no amount of good project management or skilled programming can fix a bad requirement. You may end up with an excellent piece of software that nobody wants.

A Basket of Berries

Here is a question: What do stem cells, prayer, quantum particles and berries in a basket have in common? It's kind of funny because we can lump software requirements into this question too. That's because we treat software requirements just like berries in a basket. Whenever anyone speaks about the subject of software requirements, they speak in terms of "gathering". Think about it. What other terms have you heard? Maybe, "analyzing", or "specifying" or even "designing". Nope! We "Gather Requirements" so that we can build software. When I hear or see the term "gathering" used, I sometimes think of happy children in a strawberry patch skipping from berry to berry, basket in hand, eating more than they put in their basket. When I'm in a darker mood, and I hear someone say "Gather Requirements" I think of the cave man in ancient Britannia saying , "Aye, wify, woy don't ya go out and gather us some nice berries for dinner and never mind those pesky velociraptors. If you lose another hand, you won't be much good at berry picking.. Now off with ya." The trouble with a basket of berries is that, you don't really know what they will become. They could just as easily becomes aunt Pearl's jam as well as a medication.

Intention changes everything

So what do these things listed above and gathered software requirements have in common? "Intention" that's it. They all have the potential to become many things and intention determines their outcome. What makes a stem cell turn into a skin cell rather than a cell in the back of the eye? Intention. What turns prayer from empty words into a successful outcome? Intention. What effect does intention have on a quantum particle? We'll have a look at one sometime and see what happens. Intention determines outcome. When Mr. Caveman sent his lovely bride off with an empty basket, we might wonder, what he wanted to do with the berries. He might have wanted a cherry pie and the first bush she comes upon is a black berry bush. What then? She brings home a nice basket of black berries and attempts to make her cave hubby a cherry pie. Sounds like a recipe for a bad night around the cave fire.

Beware of the Genie

What makes the story of the genie in the bottle so intriguing? We all know that when you rub the bottle and the genie escapes, that he offers three wishes to the one who released him. So what's the twist? The problem comes when the person makes a wish the genie always turns it into a bad thing for the one making the wish. The intrigue of the story is that usually, the wisher knows this and tries to outwit the genie. As the story progresses, we always discover that the intention of the wish is the hardest thing to convey and without the perfect intention, the wish always ends up a curse.

Intention changes everything. Intention turns a lump of clay into a beautiful vase. The same rock could be used as the cornerstone of a building or be carved into the lifelike image of a Greek goddess. Stem cells, prayer, quantum particles and even a basket of berries and yes, even software requirements are shaped by intention. Intention determines what becomes of these things. Unfortunately, intention is often lost when "gathering" Software requirements and they often become something other than what the customer intended. If our method is to simply gather requirements and hand them over to a software development team, what can we expect? We can expect an 85% failure rate. Without a methodology that seeks to uncover the intention of a requirement, we might as well rub the side of the genie bottle and make three wishes.

A Systemic Problem

Why is this the case? It boils down to one systemic problem. That is "the failure to communicate". This problem can be broken down into two specific areas. The first area of the problem is the failure to communicate in conversations. The second area of the problem is the failure to communicate in documentation. Let me illustrate.

A guy walks into a tool rental store and says, "I need a chain saw. I've got a lot of wood to cut and I hear that a chain saw is the tool for the job." The clerk says, "We can fix you up." In a few of minutes the happy man walks out of the store with his chain saw. A couple of hours later, the man returns to the store. He is covered in sweat, dirt and sawdust. The man says to the clerk. "Man, I thought this chain saw was gonna cut that wood like butter, but it seems harder to use than my axe." The clerk, looking puzzled, takes the chain saw from the man, sets it on the floor and pulls the rope handle on the side of the saw. The saw roars to life. The man, with a shocked look on his face , says. "What's that noise?" Face Plant, Epic Fail! What happened here? Well, as one politician put it, "What we have here is a failure to communicate."

A failure to communicate? How is that possible, the man and the clerk both knew what a chain saw looked like. Both men knew that it was used to cut wood. Both agreed that it was the right tool for a big wood cutting job. But what they did not both know was how the chain saw actually worked. Thus, the failure to communicate cost one man a day and a good deal of embarrassment for both.

Communication is a Software Designer's Job

I can sum up software design in one word... "Communication". A software designer's job is to take an idea which is sometimes vaguely identified and then communicate that idea in a way that will insure that a software developer will create it. This means that the software designer must demonstrate that he understands what the end user has requested to the end user and to the software developer.

Think about the chain saw story for a minute and relate that to a request for software. One person has a job to do. They think that job can be done more efficiently if they had a different tool. In this case, the man would like to replace his axe with a chain saw. Now, from the story, you can tell that the man did not know much about chain saws.   But, there were two things he did know. First he knew that a chain saw would be more efficient way of cutting wood than using an axe. Second, he knew where to get one. The clerk in the rental store was more than happy to supply the man with a chain saw. That was his job. His job was not to ask why the man wanted a chain saw or even to ask the man if he knew how to use one. Because it was no one's job to verify that the request would actually meet the man's need. No verification as attempted.

Now, how often does this happen in the software world? Someone has a job that they believe could be done more efficiently with a computer program. So, they ask a software developer to create one for them. No questions asked. This is what I need, and it magically gets built. The problem here is that without asking certain questions there is no way to insure that what the person asked for will actually make his job more efficient. It is a developer's job to build software. Ask one to do so and they will build a piece of software. You cannot ask a developer to satisfy the needs of customer. That is not their job. There must be a person in-between to verify that the request will satisfy the need. This takes communication between the designer and the user as well as between the designer and the developer. It involves a process of conversation and documentation. It involves a process of what my clients call Trust but Verify.

Trust But Verify

I work mostly in the Nuclear Power industry and I can tell you, they have stolen all the good words. For example, a "System" to the nuclear folks means a particular set of pipes, valves and pumps. A "Procedure" is a written document that tells them how to do a job and they can't go the rest room without a procedure. A "Program" is a set of documents that describe how they plan to comply with a certain category of government regulations. These people believe in proper communication! They have all been trained, retrained and re-re-trained to stop what they are doing if they do not understand what the next step is.

Some time ago, I was working with a large Nuclear Power company in the southeast. I will not name names to protect the guilty. They had decided to re-label everything in their plants so that it would match their procedures. As I stated, "procedures", in the nuclear world, are a printed set of steps to accomplish a task. This project was a bit more complicated than it sounds for a couple of reasons. First, they wanted the software to analyze all the equipment records stored on the mainframe, and electronically order the labels needed to re-label the plant. Secondly you can't just slap a yellow sticky note to a pipe that is 1200 degrees. Different locations throughout the plant required different kinds of labels. Some needed to be plastic, others ceramic and still others stainless steel. Thirdly, the means by which the labels were attached to the equipment was also determined by location and environment. Some were screwed on, some were hung from chains and some were strapped on with plastic ties. Finally, the quantity of these labels was well into the thousands and their arrival needed to be scheduled over time while also taking into consideration that some installations would take place in a radioactive area and the placement of those labels would have to coincide with a scheduled shutdown of the plant. All the information necessary to accomplish this task was to be found in the Company's centralized main frame. Nothing new was to be added to the mainframe. The general goal was to get the data from the mainframe, put it on a SQL Server and perform all the work from a networked PC. Once the software determined the type of labels, color, attachment and timing of the installation from the equipment data, the label specification were to be formatted to meet the criteria of the label manufacturer and sent via the internet directly to the manufacturer. As projects go, it was not too bad and kind of fun.

The project proceeded smoothly and on schedule. Before we went completely live, I produced sample orders of each kind of label along with their attachment details and sent them to the manufacturer to produce them. Once I received my order, I gathered the 20 or so people who had been assigned to implement the project from the various sites to discuss the results and get their approval to go live. Nuclear folks like to talk. It's a tight community and everyone has worked with everyone else at one time or another. When you call one of these little get-togethers it pulls in people from all over and there is a lot of catching up that goes on. It usually does not stop when you start the meeting either. The inside jokes fly around the room like love bugs during mating season. This meeting started like any other. Then I placed the new labels on the table for the team to examine. The labels were all sizes and shapes colors and materials. As the labels began to move around the room from person to person, the room got very quiet. As you might have guessed this is not a good thing. I waited several minutes as each individual held up a label and shuffled thru their written procedures to see if there was a match between the label in their hand and their written procedure.

Finally, I couldn't take it any longer. "What's wrong?" I asked. All kinds of things went thru my head. Had I not analyzed the data correctly? Had I misrepresented the colors? Had I messed up the materials? Had the system ordered the wrong kind of fasteners? Did I print the wrong information on the labels? Then one guy at the end of the table spoke. "Well, they look real nice and the material, the color and the fasteners are all good. But we can't use these. The typing is not right." "What do you mean, 'the typing in not right?'" I asked. "Well", he said, "if you look at our procedures, everything is in big letters. These labels mix big and little letters. So they don't match our procedure. So we can't use them."

The mainframe was incapable of printing lower case letters, but when I transferred all the data to the SQL Server, I converted the text to a proper case. I assumed that they wanted me to overcome the limitation of their main frame and print the labels in a more human readable font. But no, they just wanted them to match their procedures. I guess that way; a person didn't even have to be able to read to match them up. If you could match the symbols ABC found in the procedure to the ABC on the label you would know that you were looking at the correct piece of pipe or valve. Why was this so important? Well, unhook the wrong pipe or turn the wrong valve in a Nuclear Power plant some time and see what fun that kicks off. Let me show you a 500 sq. mile dead zone in Japan.

This was a failure to communicate my understanding of the requirements. I say it was a failure to <u>communicate my understanding</u> of the requirements <u>not just a failure to understand the requirements</u>. In the Nuclear world it is not enough to understand a requirement. You must also communicate it so that it can be verified. They call it "Trust but Verify". One person states an objective. The other person responds with the objective. The first person announces that the second person has correctly received the objective. This way information is not just transferred from one person to another. It is a communication loop that verifies that the two parties have successfully transferred the information.

Formalize to Simplify

I'm a pilot. In aviation, this type of communication loop is used all the time. Sometimes I want my co-pilot to take the controls. I will say to him, 'Charles, you have the airplane. Charles will say, "I have the airplane." Then, I will say, "You have the airplane." and then I release my hands from the controls. This might seem like a lot of words, but the exchange happens very quickly and effectively which I used just last week when my door popped open at 2500 feet. Not only does this work in the cockpit, it works when communicating with the Air Traffic Control. When I come in to an airport to land, I call the tower from my radio and say, *"Greenville Tower, this is Cessna 757 lima bravo, 8 miles east inbound for full stop."* The tower usually responds with *"7LB enter right base for runway one niner, you are cleared to land."* I respond, *"Enter right base for runway one niner, cleared to land. 7 lima bravo."* In this interaction, I communicated what I wanted, the controller gave me permission, then I confirmed the permission. Everybody knows what to expect and what we can and cannot do. To do this correctly and as efficiently as possible, we used the "trust but verify" communication technique but we also used very specific language designed for this type of communication. When I called the tower, my first words were *"Greenville Tower."* At my home airport, the same frequency can be used for both the tower and ground operation. By saying Greenville Tower, they knew that I wanted an interaction with them for Air movement not ground movement. Next, I said, this is *"Cessna 757 lima bravo"*. This identifies the aircraft that is calling them. We first state the type of aircraft followed by its call sign using the phonetic pronunciation. By knowing the Type of aircraft, the controller gets an idea of how fast things might be happening. In my case, my top speed is about 95 mpg so it gives them a lot of time to arrange things before I get there if they need to. By phonetically pronouncing the letters there is no mix up about what airplane they are dealing with. LE and LB sound the same on a radio but Lima Echo and Lima Bravo are clearly distinguished. Next, I told the controller where I was and lastly, I stated my request. This format is followed by all pilots coming into an airport. It doesn't matter if you are a Cessna 152 with two seats landing at a small downtown airport or a 757 full of passengers landing in Atlanta. It doesn't matter if this is the first time or the 1,000[th] time you have done this; the communication loop is the same. There is both the "trust but verify" communication technique combined with a specific language designed for the request.

Obviously, not every failure to communicate in a software project results in a smoking hole in the ground, but I guarantee that it costs money and time. Money and Time are the two things that make a business work or not work. If you run out of time, the value of what you are building can evaporate. If you run out of money, you get sent home. So, whatever the reason for a miscommunication, every miscommunication costs something. In my case, the software fix to my label ordering system was less than an hour, but the cost of reassembling the approval team was significant and caused the project completion to be delayed.

I really like the Nuclear Community. Sometimes I get frustrated with the literalism that is characteristic of Homer Simpson but I really appreciate their approach to risk mitigation in communication. "Trust but Verify" is a mantra uttered throughout the industry and it does work. I also love the aviation industry. 99% of the time, aviation communication works. We use the "trust but verify" technique and we use specific language formally designed to simplify specific requests. In both cases, communication is more successful and the risk of miscommunication is reduced. In some cases, lives are protected. In most cases, time and money are saved.

So, why not apply these same two principles to Software design. Why not use a form of "trust but verify" as well as a specific language to communicate a request. This way the end user and the developer will be in agreement. They will have the same goal in mind. They will have a common target.

Summary

1. Software projects that fail due so mostly because of incorrect requirements.

2. Incorrect Requirements are usually due to bad communication techniques.

3. The gathering of requirements and turning them over to a development team does not guarantee the result.

4. Using the "Trust but Verify" communication technique insures that both parties agree that the information has been successfully transferred between them.

5. Using a formal specific language for a repetitive communication task will reduce miscommunication.

Chapter 2: The land before time

It's not rocket science... Or is it?

Even at the dawn of the computer age, we find major efforts to solve this problem. The following story explains how we got so far off track and how even the attempt to communicate the solution failed to communicate.

In 1970 Dr. Winston W. Royce had been working over the previous nine years on the development of software packages for spacecraft mission planning, commanding and post-flight analysis. In other words, he was a rocket scientist. In August of that year, at a meeting of the Institute of Electrical and Electronic Engineers (IEEE) he presented a paper called "Managing the Development of Large Software Systems." (Royce, 1970) In his opening remarks he states that "there are two essential steps common to all computer program developments, regardless of size or complexity. There is first an analysis step, followed second by a coding step." He illustrates this with the following simple diagram.

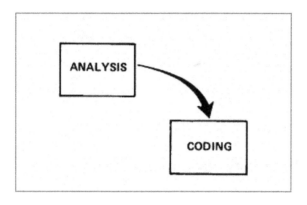

Figure 1 (Royce's First Figure)

Royce goes on to say that these two steps are usually all that is required for a simple project or software intended to be used in-house. But, for a larger system, one that is built for a client, more steps are required. It is interesting that he states that most customers are happy to pay for the two-step method "Since both steps involve genuinely creative work which directly contributes to the usefulness of the final product" He then says. "An implementation plan to manufacture larger software systems, and keyed only to these steps, however, is doomed to failure."

Royce goes on to say, "Many additional development steps are required, none contribute as directly to the final product as analysis and coding, and all drive up the development costs. Customer personnel typically would rather not pay for them, and development personnel would rather not implement them. The prime function of management is to sell these concepts to both groups and then enforce compliance on the part of development personnel."

Royce says, "The analysis and coding steps are still in the picture, but they are preceded by two levels of requirements analysis, are separated by a program design step, and followed by a testing step."

Royce then introduces the other steps in the following illustration:

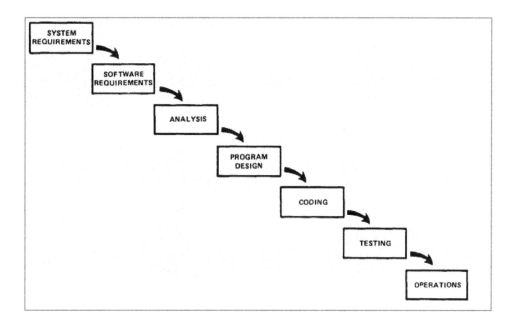

Figure 2 (Royce's figure 2)

The figure is labeled "Implementation steps to develop a large computer program for delivery to a customer."

There never was a waterfall

I firmly believe that when this paper was released to the general public everyone stopped reading it right here. This is the classic definition of the "Waterfall Method". The assumption being that these "Steps" are to be completed in succession before moving to the next. Thus a waterfall effect. This could not be further from what Dr. Royce was saying. The very next sentence following this illustration is this. "I believe in this concept, but the implementation described above is risky and invites failure."

Royce introduces his third illustration with these words: " Figure 3 portrays the iterative relationship between successive development phases for this scheme. The ordering of steps is based on the following concept: that as each step progresses and the design is future detailed, there is an iteration with the preceding and succeeding steps but rarely with the more remote steps in the sequence."

Do you catch his meaning? In 1970 this man said, that **design was detailed over the course of the steps**, not in one step. He is saying that there is iteration of the steps. This is NOT A WATERFALL!

Here is his Figure 3:

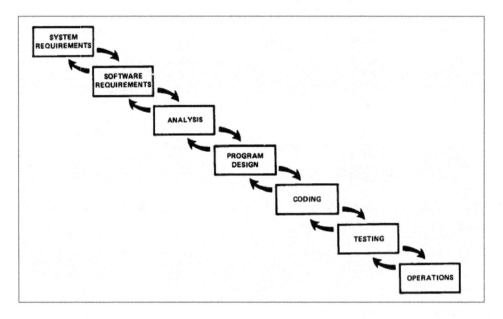

Figure 3 (Royce's Figure 3)

Royce notes that it would be nice if each iterative interaction between the steps was confined to success steps but he immediately introduces the following illustration to show that it is not so.

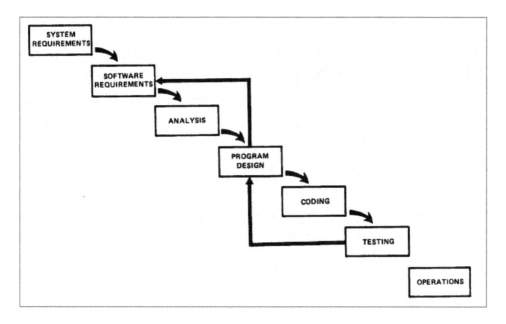

Figure 4 (Royce's Figure 4)

This illustration is clearly indicating that this iteration the interaction can move beyond the preceding or successive steps.

He concludes his paper with 5 overarching steps as follows:

1. Program Design Comes First
2. Document the Design
3. Do it Twice (prototype, then build the real thing)
4. Plan Control and Monitor Testing
5. Involve the Customer ("-the involvement should be formal, in-depth, and continuing.")

The final illustration in the paper is this:

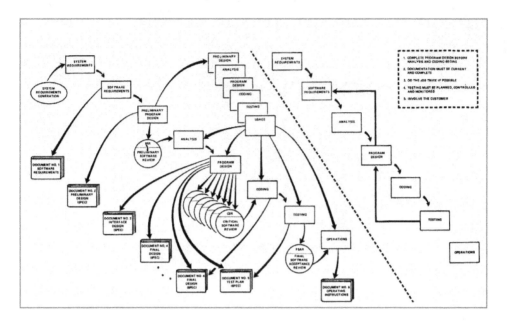

Figure 5 (Royce's Final Summary Illustration)

Paralyzed by Analysis

So how in the world did the software community get stuck on this 'Waterfall Idea'? The paper clearly defines an iterative process where steps are repeated and design grows with the software. He clearly states that documentation is paramount but not less important than continuous customer involvement that is "formal, in-depth and continuing." How is it possible that in the decades that followed this paper, software projects were buried in paper, paralyzed by analysis and excluded the customer until the final product was delivered where it ran into 300% overruns, was so late it was obsolete and was not at all what the customer asked for in the first place. More than one study showed that 95% all software projects in the 1990's failed by being over budget, late or were just canceled.

In his book SDLC 3.0 Beyond a Tacit Understanding of Agile, Mark Kennaley (Kennaley, 2010) speculates "that the articulation was taken the wrong way for what one could assume are reasons of simplicity, or worse – the ability to delay the day of reckoning by projects that were doomed to fail." Interesting! For whatever the reason for the misunderstanding, the idea persists to this day and is the straw man that every other software methodologist must attack. As late as 2003, I was handed a three inch think binder by one of my clients outlining how their particular Nuclear Facility would implement all software development and it followed the Waterfall diagram to a tee. Not only was this a standard. It was considered the best of standards as this company was named in the InformationWeek 500 Magazine's annual list of U.S. companies with the best technology and business practices that year!

As the Waterfall Method took a stranglehold on software development in the 80's and '90's more and more middle management was called upon to control the process because of the extreme number of failed projects. Proof that a "step" in the process was completed was pounds of documentation. Tools were developed to gauge the progress of the waterfall but to no avail. Projects still failed.

Introduction of the Use Case

In 1985, working on his PHD thesis called "Language Constructs for Large Real Time Systems" , Ivar Jacobson invented a way of documenting software process by making a kind of blueprint. This was the first step toward formalizing the language of software requirements. For requirements definitions, he invented the **Use Case**. The Use Case describes the context of a request and lays out specific scenarios that the request will follow. It finishes by describing what the completed state of the request would look like. In the early '90s, Jacobson joined with two other methodologists; Grady Booch and James Rumbaugh to form a company called Rational.

Introduction of RUP

Rational created a new methodology called RUP which was an acronym for the "Rational Unified Process." What was "unified" about the process was that the work of these three methodologist (Jacobson, Booch, and Rumbaugh)[2] was combined into a single process. This methodology rejected the idea that all software requirements could be documented before the code could begin and then introduced two solutions. The first solution was that software documentation should include diagrams not just words. The second solution was that software development should be incremental and iterative. Maybe these guys just read Royce's paper. Modeling worked. Incremental and iterative development worked. More software was written correctly than ever before. But middle management did not go away and neither did the "Waterfall" mentality. Rational made its money on tools which were very expensive. The RUP grew to include "over 35 overly specialized roles, 99 or so artifacts/work products which were commonly manifested as documents, and a work breakdown structure that contained over 174 or so activities..." (Kennaley, 2010). In other words, the RUP tools became a project unto itself. Poorly trained users and the complexity of the RUP tools brought things to a halt once again.

The Agile Manifesto

Is it any wonder that a few outspoken methodologists got together in Feb. 2001 and rebelled against this insanity? While meeting at a ski resort in Utah, 17 men with varying degrees of management and practitioner experience drew up what they called the "Agile Manifesto" Here is the exact web page they published;
http://agilemanifesto.org/

---

[2] **http://en.wikipedia.org/wiki/IBM_Rational_Unified_Process**

Here are the exact words of the manifesto in its entirety:

We are uncovering better ways of
developing software by doing it and
helping others do it.
Through this work we have come to value:

Individuals and interactions over
processes and "tools,
Working software over
comprehensive documentation,
Customer collaboration over
contract negotiation,
Responding to change over
following a plan.

That is, while there is value in the items on
the right, we value the items on the left
more."

The miserable "Waterfall Method" had ruled the software community for 30 years. RUP came to the rescue in an attempt to formalize the conversation but quickly turned into a mountain of paperwork. The knee-jerk reaction by the Agilest was to through the baby out with the bath water. Agile Methodology emphasized less dependence upon tools and process, to allow software developers to react more quickly to ever-changing requirements. Streamlining the process and conversation with the customer became paramount. The RUP was too heavy a burden to bear and was rejected for real just-in-time conversations, very little documentation and no plan or estimate for project completions. Others began to chime in.

Lean Practices

Lean Methodology or Practices were borrowed from Toyota's manufacturing process and were introduced to the software community in 2006, with a book called Implementing Lean Software Development – from Concept to Cash by Mary and Tom Poppendieck. (Poppendieck, 2006) The main emphasis of the Lean Methodology is the reduction of waste in the process. The process makes people more cognoscente of documentation and activities that add no value to the process. By dumping things that add no value, the process should move forward faster.

Scrum

Scrum[3] is a form of project management that incorporates both Agile and Lean practices. (Shalloway, 2009) With Scrum, a backlog of requirements or "features", mostly described as "User Stories", drive the process. Development efforts are limited in time to usually less than a month.

So, the software community has come a long way from the "Waterfall" days but the fact remains, projects fail and they mostly fail because of incorrect requirements. Why is that? The real problems of communication had not been solved. The formal documentation process of the RUP was an attempt to create a language specific to the problems of software design but was turned into a documentation kingdom and then rejected. Granted, agile methodologies shortened development cycles but the end result was only a clearer picture of what not to build. In the end the Agile rebellion could no more guarantee predictable results than any of its predecessors.

---

[3] http://en.wikipedia.org/wiki/Scrum_(development)

Recent Thought

Over the years, many methods have been tried to insure that software projects accomplish their goals. Recently thought leaders (Jacobson 2012) [4]have been rethinking the progress of software development methodologies. I believe they are now saying that the combination of the best of these methods can produce predictable results. The two areas of communication failure are in conversation and in documentation. If the conversation can be guided by specific language designed for the task of clarifying software requirements and the documentation can be simple, streamlined and clear enough to be just enough information for the development team, we just might have the best of both worlds.

Where to start?

If we are going to solve the problem of incorrect requirements we must treat them like a communication problem. We must borrow the "Trust but Verify" technique from the nuclear community and take a queue form the aviation industry and use a Formal language designed for the task.

The Use Case is the Formal Language

In the Agile methodology, used in many shops today, there is a very simple tool for capturing requirements. It is called the User Story. It does use a specific language designed to fit the process but the User Story is not to be confused with a Use Case. The User Story is really nothing more than a request for some software function. It is said to be "a reminder to have a conversation later." In other words, the User Story is

---

[4] Succeeding with Agile @ Scale Conference, London March 8, 2012

a place holder for a software idea. Dean Leffingwell, in his book <u>Agile Software Requirements </u>(Leffingwell, 2011) says this about User Stories,

> "Simply put, although a nice itemized list of backlog items is easy to look at, tool, prioritize, and manage, it is inadequate to do the more complex analysis work that larger systems require. And even though we've called our back log items User stories, they don't really tell much of a story after all, at least not one much beyond what a casual reader might understand."

Lefdingwell, goes on to say that right answer is to elaborate the User Story with standard UML Use Cases. Lefdingwell refers to Alistair Cockburn, an agile thought leader and one of the signers of the Agile Manifesto who actually agrees with exactly this point. Cockburn, on his web site says this:

> "XP[5] pretty much banned Use Cases, replacing them with the similar sounding 'User Stories' and as a result agile zealots have been happy to dump Use Cases in the trash (along with their project managers, estimates, plans, and architectures). Scrum did similar, using the "product backlog" instead of User stories. Yet as I go around projects, I keep running across organizations suffering from three particular, real, painful, and expensive problems."

In summary, Cockburn describes the three problems as 1. The User Story lacks context. 2. The User Story lacks detail and 3. The User Story lacks completeness. He says that the lack of context means that when the programmer is presented with a User Story, they do not know where the request will fit in the larger picture or who else might use the same function. He says the lack of detail leads to bad estimates because there are always details left out of the story. A story that seems simple on the surface seems to grow without bounds as the development process begins and the programmer discovers more and more about the request. Finally, Cockburn says that the fact that there is no context and no detail, the User Story gives the programmer no idea when things will really be done. There is no scope or scale to a set of stories. There could be stories in the backlog that could take months. No one knows until after estimates are given and work has begun that the true size and

---

[5] XP = Extreme Programing methodology that pairs two programs and a customer for a project.

complexity of a request is discovered. He says that this causes discouragement for both the programmer and the customer.

In conclusion, Cockburn says "In particular, Use Cases fix those three problems." (Cockrun)

Scott Ambler, a thought leader in the Agile community, says "... Use Case diagrams overview the usage requirements for a system. They are useful for presentations to management and/or project stakeholders, but for actual development you will find that Use Cases provide significantly more value because they describe "the meat" of the actual requirements."[6]

If the User Story is a reminder to have a conversation, then what is that conversation? How is it documented? Who agrees to the answers that come from that conversation? Unfortunately, that conversation is not usually a single conversation. Sometimes it is many conversations with answers, sometimes taking weeks to be addressed. Often, no documentation comes from these conversations. Elaborating each User Story and documenting the results in a Use Case gives the entire team a better view of what they are building. This will improve estimates and delivery.

At the heart of the Feature Model is a Use Case diagram. It begins with a request for "Feature" then each User Story that might emerge from the feature is written out. After these are completed, detailed steps or tasks to complete are documented as "requirements." This information is then combined into a Use Case diagram that identifies the context of the feature. The Use Case includes both the possible Users and the possible locations within the larger application. Each scenario that the feature will take is documented in the Use Case. The model includes the domains and data that the feature uses or changes. The picture is completed when the Use Case describes what "done" looks like for the feature.

---

[6] **http://www.agilemodeling.com/artifacts/useCaseDiagram.htm**

Trust but Verify is Iterative

The Trust but Verify process is implemented by using the Feature Model as a communication tool. It is intended for both the end user and the development team. Looking at Royce's diagram one more time we can see that we are targeting the problem of requirements at the beginning of the process, but it does not end there.

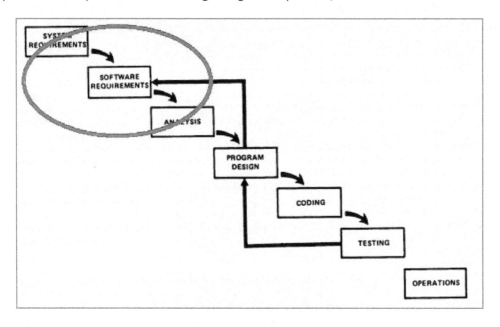

Figure 6 The Feature Model Target is Requirements

Program Design that takes place in the development process and testing that takes place after the software is constructed. Both feed back information to the requirements. This is why the Feature Model contains test plans. The test plans give direction to the testers as to how to approach the testing of the feature as well as the details of the tests themselves. The goal of testing is not just to prove that the software works. The end goal of testing is to verify that the requirements were met.

The Trust but Verify process is a learning and evolving process. Requirements are not some Rosetta stone that all else is judged by. Requirements are fluid and change with feedback. This is why the Feature Model is not static and can be modified by program design and testing feedback.

This is not a return to the Waterfall.

I am not falling back to the Waterfall and saying everything must be documented before coding begins. I am not introducing 174 steps or 100 artifacts either. I believe the answer is to construct a simple software model for each requirement. I call this **The Feature Model**. The Feature Model will explore these questions for each request. This modeling cannot be done in an ad-hoc manner by asking questions of the customer on the fly. The customer must be focused on answering this set of questions for each feature they request. The modeler should have a working knowledge of the entire system including the UI standards and business knowledge about the product. The modeler should work with the customer one-on-one to get these models done. This means that a short amount of time is spent with the customer so the questions can be considered. The modeler then creates the model and presents it to the customer. The customer can now visualize their request. They approve it and the Feature Model goes into the backlog. The models would be made public as a website for the entire team including technical writers, testers and support personnel giving the entire view of what is to come.

The models are straight forward with strict standards to improve communication. Modules should not take a long time to build. Models deal only with **What** the customer wants, **not How** the developer will build it.

This is not a return to RUP.

This is not a disguised attempt at making a RUP kingdom. There is only one artifact produced. That is a single model of a single feature that may encompass one or more User Stories. The model is published as a web site so all team members have access to it.

The Following Chapters Describe the Feature Model

In the following chapters, I will describe the Feature Model. This document does not go into detail about how to build a model but does go into detail about how to read and navigate the model. The model makes use of standard UML (unified modeling language) diagrams, Use Cases, Screen Mockups and the like. By introducing the Feature Model at the front end of the Development Process, developers will be freed from having to track down the customer for details. This does not preclude development teams from having access to the customer, but reduces wasted time for both the developer and the customer. My goal is to set a standard that will be useful to all team members and move everyone to a happier, more profitable bottom line.

Summary

1. Analysis and Code work for small in-house projects, but for larger systems, using only these two steps will fail.

2. There must be an interactive and incremental process around the analysis and code phases of the project.

3. To solve the Requirements we need the Trust but Verify communication technique as well as a formal language designed for software requirements that simplifies the communication.

4. User Stories lack context, detail and completeness.

5. Elaborating User Stories into Use Cases will bring a standard language to the software requirements as well as a level of detail that will allow customer and programmer to agree.

6. The Feature Model presents a comprehensive view of a Software Requirement that evolves with design and testing.

7. Testing proves not just that the software works but that the software built, meets the requirements.

Chapter 3: What's a Feature Model?

"There is nothing so useless as doing efficiently that which should not be done at all." Peter Drucker

The Feature

The Feature is a request for some piece of software. Usually the request is stated in simple "sales like" terms. You can think of a feature like something a salesman might pitch to a potential customer. A Feature is the general idea of something the User would consider to have value, expressed in the User's terms. Features are the building blocks of any software system and set the pace for development. "Features are the essential planning units for releases, what the development team uses to decide what is done and when." (Shalloway, 2009)[7] . Shalloway further defines a feature as follows: *"A feature is a business function that the product carries out."* [8]

The Model

The Model is a repository for what can be known about a feature before and after it is built. In some ways, the software model is like a blue print of a house. In others, it

---

[7] Pg 45

[8] Pg 179

is like the plastic model of an airplane. A blue print of a house is made up of different sets of diagrams. There are structural diagrams and electrical diagrams and pluming diagrams. Like a blue print, the software model uses different sets of diagrams with specialized symbols to describe different attributes of the software and can get extremely detailed. These diagrams are grouped by their type. Data diagrams are grouped into a set called a Data Model. Testing Diagrams are group into a set called a Test Model. Think about an airplane model. The model airplane is made up of many smaller parts which are actually models of other things like a wing or a wheel. Together, all the small models become a single model of an airplane. The software model is like the model airplane in that it is made up of a series of smaller models that represent different ideas. With the airplane model, all the smaller models add up to one airplane model. A software model is the sum of various kinds of smaller models that represent different ideas. Together all these idea models become one whole software model.

The Purpose of the Feature Model

Models can evolve with a project and become an important source of documentation for understanding and maintaining a system long after it is deployed. A software model can include everything about a piece of software from its inception to its deployment. But, the "Feature" Model does not cover as much ground. The purpose of the Feature Model is to capture what the User is asking for. This being the case, the Feature Model does not attempt to document the design of the software itself. Rather, it is a model of the request. The Feature Model may contain User Stories, Use Cases, Requirements Details, Activity Diagrams, Data Models and UI (User Interface) Mock-Ups. The Feature Model becomes the basis for development as well as the basis for critical documentation such as Acceptance Test Plans and User Guides. The Feature Model acts as the bridge between the one requesting software and the one developing the software in terms that they both can understand and agree to.

Sturcture of the Feature Modle

As stated above, the software model is made up of a serices of smaller models each represeintg different ideas or details about the software. The Feature model is made up of seven distinct models; Business Process Model, Requirements Model, Use Case Model, Domain Model, Data Model, Test Model and the User Interface Model.

Lean Thinking

How does a Feature Model foster lean thinking? The basic idea of Lean Thinking is to shorten the time from "Concept to Cash" by applying some tried and true principles as laid out by Mary and Tom Poppendieck, authors of Implementing Lean Software Development – from Concept to Cash. (Poppendieck, 2006) According to the Poppendiecks the current set of principles are: (Poppendieck.LLC)

- Optimize the Whole
- Eliminate Waste
- Build Quality In
- Learn Constantly
- Deliver Fast
- Engage Everyone

Modeling is not the answer to every one of these principles but it does contribute greatly to the effort.

Modeling Reduces wasted time.

The modeling effort involves the Modeler and the Customer discussing what to build. This one on one interaction replaces lengthy and redundant conversations between members of the development team and the customer about what to build. As this may seem to violate one of the tenants of Xp[9], it does not. What to build is a business

---

[9] Extreme Programming

decision, not a technical one. Detailed design questions are still dealt with between the team and the customer. Modeling makes more efficient use of both the Customer's and Developers' time. It frees the developer from the inception phase of a project allowing them to concentrate on construction. Modeling assists the customer in visualizing a concept. The customer's time is spent on ideas. The ideas are modeled and then verified. Models take less time to build than code. This shortens the feedback loop between idea and its verification. Instead of waiting weeks to view working code, the customer can examine a model within days of the original discussion giving them time to consider the value of the idea before involving the development team.

Modeling Reduces wasted code.

Requiring a model to be built before code, allows the customer time to consider the value and the impact of the request before spending money on code that will cost too much, take too long to build or bring little value to the customer. In Developer-to-Customer conversations, the conceptual feedback comes in the form of Code that may be tossed. By visualizing a concept, many details can be cleared up before unusable code is created.

Modeling Serves the Whole Team.

When code is developed with the involvement of only the customer and the developer, other team members are left in the dark. A model allows testers, technical writers and support staff to be involved in the process. This allows everyone to be ready for a release when the code is finished rather than scrambling to discover what just got built.

Modeling allows a clear picture of progress.

As models are developed and code is completed, the team gains a clearer picture of the overall scope of the project. This will enable the team to have a basis for estimating the time to completion. The backlog of models allows for better release planning by picking the most marketable features first.

Modeling Improves Quality

With a model, the technical writers and testers have a guide to insure quality. Rather than running new code to discover what it does, they verify the quality of new code by insuring that it meets specific requirements outlined in the model.

What or How? That is the question.

There are two parts to any software project: what and how. The "what" part of this equation is looking for a solution to what the client wants. Do they want a screen of data? Do they want a report? Do they want some unseen function that will change the data they have stored in the database?

The "how" part of this equation is looking for the implementation of the "what"? In other words, how do I make the "what" work? The "how" involves everything from which language you use to develop the software to the every line of code written. The Feature Model does not deal with the "how" software gets built. The Feature Model deals only with "What" is built. The Feature Model is a model of what the User wants in the context of what they have.

The Four Questions of What

There are four "whats" that the Feature Model is addressing. "What permissions do the various Users need? What is the context? What kind of interaction do the Users want? What information will the Users work with?

1.   What Permissions are needed?

Considering what permissions are needed for various Users, requires an understanding of the Users in their specific context. Often there is more than one kind of User involved. So, in the model, User definitions are explored to determine the best possible combinations of permissions for each User. Looking at this does not simply mean "Create", "Edit", "Print" or "View." It also involves looking at the navigation path for the desired functions. If, for example, one User has permission to print a certain set of data, but they do not have permission to create the data, they also may be restricted from even seeing what another User sees. This could affect what menu options are available to Users. The Use Case clears this up by Actor definitions and scenarios.

2.   What is the greater Context?

When considering any feature, it must be recognized that it will become part of a larger whole. Sometimes a feature requires a single entry point. Other times, the feature is something that will be used from different locations within the larger system. This usually invoices the simple question, "where does this feature launch from?" It can also involve the more complex question of what other features might this one be related to. This is often lost when only User Stories are pulled from a backlog. It might make sense to deploy this feature with a related one. This will not only affect where it will be implemented but also when it will be developed.

3.   What Interaction is expected?

"What interaction" deals with the User's interface with the software? This can include the layout of screens and reports as well as navigation paths through the system. It involves the look and feel of the software, as well as feedback the User receives from the system, and immediate help made available to the User. Basically, the entire experience of the use of the software is captured in the Feature Model so that everyone involved knows where the software is going and how to test it when it is done. This part of the model is handled primarily by the scenarios of the Use Case.

4.   What Information will be manipulated?

Software is mostly about information. It almost always involves the movement, grouping, analyzing, storing and retrieving information. That information is what the User sees on the screens and on the reports. Sometimes this involves actions that the User does not see such as reformatting or applying certain formulas. The Feature Model captures the details of that information and what must be done with that information to accomplish the User's goal. This part of the Feature Model is made up of notes, domain models, data models and Robustness Diagrams.

Summary:

1. A Feature is a requested piece of software that a customer perceives to have some business value. It is work that a specific Development team can accomplish in a specified amount of time agreed upon by both the Client and the Development team.

2. A Feature Model is the representation of what the User has requested and is not the design of the software that will be built. The Feature Model addresses four basic questions:
   - What permissions will be needed for various Users?
   - What is the larger context of the feature?
   - What interaction does the User expect to have with the software?
   - What information will be manipulated by this request?

3. The Feature Model fosters Lean Development by:
   a. Reducing wasted time
   b. Reducing wasted code
   c. Serving the whole Team
   d. Allowing a clear Picture of progress
   e. Improving Quality

Chapter 4: What's in a Feature Model?

The Presentation of the Model

Developing a model can be as simple as drawing on a white board or as complicated as using a $30,000 modeling tool. Using the white board involves drawing the models on a white board and taking photos of the board for review at a later time. Though cost effective, this may not be the best way to capture the ideas, especially if they have to be presented to a client. This approach works best when modeling a quick question about the design of the software. Again, the Feature Model is not dealing with the design but the request. So, organizing and keeping the models on hand, extracting the relevant portions into User Guides and Test Plans cannot be done by writing on a whiteboard. There are various tools that can be used. Enterprise Architect® or "EA" from Sparx Systems[10] is a very inexpensive and very comprehensive tool. EA allows the modeler to develop the model in an organized fashion and present pieces and parts of the model in RTF or Web format. The web presentation of the model is interactive and allows the viewer to drill down into the details. In this book, all illustrations come from the Web format.

A Model is the representation of the software requested. It is presented as a series diagrams using standard UML notation. The model forms the basis for development and documentation. Once completed, the Model is published as a web page.

------

[10] **www.sparxsystems.com**

The web presentation is convenient because it can be published so all members of a team have access to it and updates can be given to the team immediately. The model is made up of two main components. First, there is a navigation tree view on the left hand side of the web page. Second, there is a display area to the right of the tree view where the diagrams are displayed. Each symbol on each diagram may have additional details associated with it. A single symbol can also have an entirely separate diagram associated with it. The navigation to this additional information is done by clicking on any symbol in any diagram. The tree view allows the user to navigate to any diagram in the model

The actual contents of a Feature Model can be grouped into six major components; the "Feature Statement", the Use Case Model, the Domain Model, the Data Model, the User Interface Model and the Test Plans. The Feature Statement is a single clear statement describing the request. The various models may involve more than one diagram based on the complexity of the request.

For convenience, these components are grouped onto a single page called the Feature Model Summary that allows quick access to these sections in the Feature Model.

Opening the first element of the tree view will reveal a node called the Feature Model Summary. Clicking on this node will display the six major components of the Feature Model. All navigation can then be accomplished by clicking on the symbols on the Feature Model Summary rather than hunting through the tree view.

The Feature Model Summary

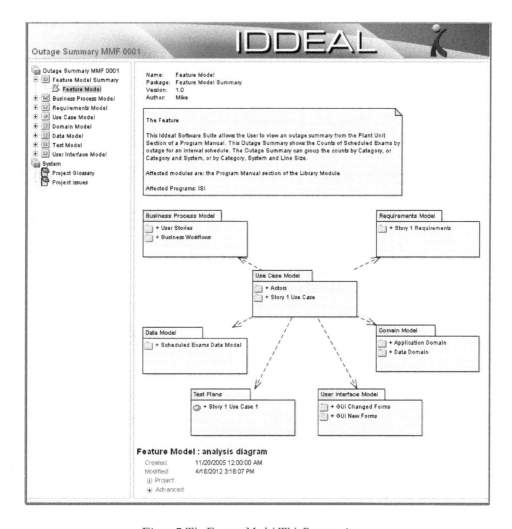

Figure 7 The Feature Model Web Presentation

As you can see in the figure above, there is a tree view on the left, used to navigate the model and the actual model diagrams appear to the right of the tree view. The web presentation of these diagrams is interactive. The diagrams are designed to allow anyone to navigate through them by clicking directly on the symbols in the diagram. The model is built in layers and has different sections to address different ideas. Those layers can be found under the different sections of the tree view. The root nodes in the tree view represent different types of models. These are depicted as a manila square with a symbol in the center. The symbol represents the type of model in that section. Each model may have one or many diagrams associated with it. All of this information is contained in folders or "packages" that are noted on the tree view as a manila folder.

In this presentation, the entire model has been summarized into one page called the Feature Model Summary. All of the relevant information can be obtained by clicking on the Feature Model Summary that is shown in the work space to the right of the tree view.

To open the model, the viewer clicks on the Feature Model Summary Node to open the first tree view section and then clicks on the Feature Model Symbol.

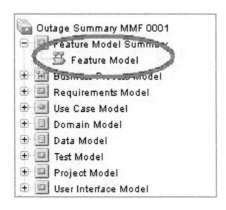

Figure 8 Click to Open the Model

At the top of the summary page is the Feature statement. The Feature statement is presented as a note and is complete as it appears. No drill-down is necessary to read the Feature statement. The rest of the symbols shown on the Feature Model Summary represent folders within the model. Each of the folders contains different parts of the model. These folders are Business Process Model, Requirements Model, Use Case Model, Domain Models, Data Models, User Interface Models and Test Plans. Each of these sections will be explained in the following chapters.

Basically, the Feature Statement is a summary of the request. The Business Process Model introduces the main ideas behind the feature in the form of User Stories and Business Flow diagrams. The Requirements model expands the User Stories into requirements or steps to complete a story. The Use Cases describe the interaction between the User and the software. The Domain model describes where the request fits into the bigger picture. The Data model describes the information that will be used or changed by the request. The User Interface model describes what the feature will look like to the User. And, finally, the Test Plans contain valuable notes for those who will have to prove the quality of the competed software.

The Feature Model is a Bridge

There are many parts to a Feature Model. The key thing to remember about a Feature Model is that it is a bridge between two parties. On the one side is the Client with ideas, expectations and money. On the other side, is the Developer with skill, technique and time. In order to bring these two parties together, a vision that they both can agree to must be created. The model is just that. It is a model of an idea. It is not the completed working software. It has been suggested that software be built with the User and the Developer sitting side by side, writing the software until the desired request suddenly materializes before them. This may be one way to accomplish a software request but not the most practical. Users usually have real jobs that preclude their attention to a software project. Developers often want facts, commitments and real ideas that can be coded, rather than possibilities, that once built, are just thrown away. And those paying for all this just want the job done in the most efficient and cost-effective way possible.

The Feature Model is a Visualization of a Request

The Feature Model is a tool used to allow two parties to visualize the request. Client and Developers never work at the same pace. So, there is a modeler who works between them spending at much time with each party separately to move them to the point of agreement. If the model can be standardized, the time spent with the Developer is minimized. Once the User "sees" the vision and says "Yes, this is what I want." The model can then presented to the Developers, questions get addressed, the model is modified and the final agreement between both parties is reached. Then the building process can begin.

A key point here is that the model does not tell a Developer how to make a piece of software. It simply lays out what the User expects the software to do.

A Feature Module should be Light

A Feature Model, by its nature is meant to be light, simple, uncomplicated. In the past, some have made models so complex that they became projects unto themselves and have hindered the progress of many software projects. The Feature Model is a model of a feature - not a model of an application. Some, in the past, have tried to model entire systems or applications before building anything. As we all know, that approach was doomed to failure. The Feature Model concentrates on a single Feature, not the whole of a system.

A Feature Model Represents a Work project.

The Feature Model represents a work project that can be accomplished in a relatively short amount of time. Software development is not something that should go on and on forever. Like any project, goals must be set, metrics must be analyzed and schedules must be met. Many ideas about software development have emerged in recent years. One such idea is that development is done in short bursts of time. This is called a "Sprint." The length of time actually given to a Sprint, and the number of developers involved is determined by each development team itself. But, many have suggested that a three week development cycle is a good target.

The Feature Model is a bridge between the User and the Development Team. But it is not a bridge to just any development team. To be effective, the model must be tailored to match the Sprint of the targeted Development team. The amount of work envisioned within a single Feature Model should be something that can be accomplished in one Sprint of that development team. If the model envisions more work than can be accomplished by that team's Sprint, then the model should be broken down into smaller models.

The Feature Model Structure

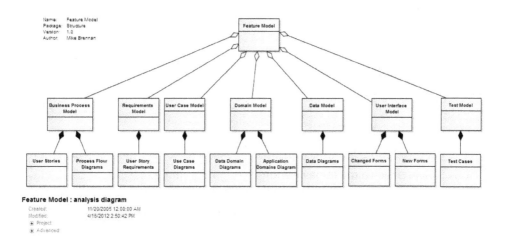

The Feature model is made up of seven folders of diagrams. Each folder is referred to as a model. Each model has a specific kind of diagram associated with it.

Summary

1. The Feature Model Presentation is best delivered in a web format that is interactive and allows the viewer to drill down into the various pieces and parts.

2. The Feature Model is made up of seven major components which are summarized on the Feature Summary Page. Those components are:
    -The Business Process Model
    - The Requirements Model
    -The Use Case Model
    - The Domain Model
    - The Data Model
    - The User Interface
    - The Test Plans

3. The Feature Model Summary groups the seven major components together on a single page to make navigation through the model easy.

4. The Feature Model is a communication bridge between the Customer and the Developer and allows both parties to visualize the request.

5. Feature Models are designed to be quick to build and easy to read.

6. The Feature Model represents a piece of work that can be accomplished in a single development cycle called a Sprint.

Chapter 5: Background of this Example

There is no Vacuum

Whenever a model is developed, it is not done so in a vacuum. There is always a context that both the Requester and the Developer understand. Throughout this document, the particular model used to introduce the general principles, pieces and parts of the Feature Model is for a feature of a much larger system. In this case, the software application was developed by Iddeal® Concepts, Inc.[11] for the Nuclear Power industry to assist in the planning and execution of inspections of individual components of the power plant. These plans are contained in a document called a Program Manual. There are different "Programs" placed in Program Manuals such as the In-Service Inspection Program or ISI. The plans in these manuals include the components to be inspected, the types of inspections to be performed and the timing of the inspections. These Program Manuals are broken down into sections. One of those sections is the Plant Unit Section. A "Plant" refers to a specific location of a facility. A "Unit" refers to one reactor at that facility. In the Plant Unit Section, a User can find all of the inspections for a given Plant Unit. Many inspections are performed when the power plant unit is shut down. This down time is called an "Outage."

---

[11] http://www.iddeal.com/

Normally, none of this information is outlined in a Feature Model because it is already understood by both the Requester and the Development team. If a term is new to either, that term may be discussed in the Feature Statement or as an entry in the model's glossary.

Navigating the Model

The Web presentation of the model allows the User to navigate down in to more detail by clicking on any symbol on the page. The model does not provide backward navigation. To go back to a previous page, the User must use the "back" button on the web browser.

Chapter 6: The Feature Statement

The Feature Statement is shown at the top of the Feature Model Summary page as a note.

> **The Feature**
>
> This Iddeal Software Suite allows the User to view an outage summary from the Plant Unit Section of a Program Manual. This Outage Summary shows the Counts of Scheduled Exams by outage for an interval schedule. The Outage Summary can group the counts by Category, or Category and System, or by Category, System and Line Size.
>
> Affected modules are: the Program Manual section of the Library Module
>
> Affected Programs: ISI

Figure 9 The Feature Statement

Sales-Like Language

The statement describes, in sales-like language, what the request is. Below this statement are more important notes. These notes relate to the context of the request as it relates to an existing or developing system. A feature is usually only a small part of a larger system. Where in that system a particular request might fit can be stated in simple terms as shown in the above figure, but sometimes, describing this context may require a separate layer.

Unique Id

In this feature, the User is asking to view something called an Outage Summary. This also has become the title of the model itself. It is helpful to give a Feature a unique identifier so that it can be referenced in other documents such a Kanban[12] board or test plans. In this model, the title includes the unique identifier "MMF 001." In this example, MMF stands for Minimum Marketable Feature but how a feature is identified is really up to the team.

Common Knowledge Must be Common

As you read thru the feature statement, it becomes more specific. The placement of the request within the larger system is "from the Plant Unit Section of a Program Manual" This assumes that everyone who will be reading this model knows what a "Plant Unit Section of a Program Manual" means. If this is not the case, more details may be needed. If you look at the full tree view section in Figure 1, you will see that there is a section at the bottom of the tree called "Glossary." This section contains definitions of what the modeler considers to be unfamiliar terms.

---

[12] Kanban board- A project management tool

Narrow the Scope

The feature statement finishes up with remarks about specific data that will be used. This is expressed in laymen's terms as if it came from the User. The feature statement is meant to establish the scope of the request, not all of the specific details. The details emerge as the model is developed.

Following the Feature Statement is a couple of more notes. The first note establishes that the request is for a specific module of the software system. This information is helpful when dealing with a large system that has many modules. This note establishes a location within the larger system and would imply navigation and permission requirements.

The final note is very specific to the software application being developed. In this case, the "ISI Program" is one of many kinds of Program Manuals that can be held in this software application. Again, this is also something that only has value if the User and the Development team understand the meaning of this statement. In this context, this feature has been limited to a very narrow scope within a very large system.

Match the Sprint

The goal of a feature statement is to set the scope of a project. The scope of that project should be something that the development team can complete within a single iteration, Sprint or programming phase. In other words, if the development team usually sets a pace of three weeks to complete a unit of work, the feature should be something that can be completed within three weeks. If, however, after the feature is elaborated or the development team has estimated the effort to be more than its development cycle, then the entire model should be broken down into smaller pieces that fit the pace of the team.

Summary

1. The Feature statement describes what the customer wants in "sales like" language.

2. The Feature has a unique Id and a title.

3. The Feature statement describes something that can be done in one development "Sprint" or development cycle.

4. The Feature Model is an elaboration of the Feature.

Chapter 7: Elaborating the Feature

Stories

The building of a Feature Model is a process of elaborating the request. This is done in deliberate stages and summarized at various levels. For example, the first step in elaborating a Feature is to identify the potential Users or "Actors." The second step is to write simple User Stories for the potential Users. This is followed by enumerating the requirements implied by each User Story. There may be one or many requirements generated from one User Story. The next step is to develop the flow of the interaction between the User and the Software in a Use Case. One or more User Stories may be related to one Use Case.

Summarize the Details

At this point, the information is summarized by linking the Actors, User Stories, and Requirements to the Use Cases in a summary diagram in a folder called Use Case Model. This folder is then linked to the Feature Summary Page.

Model the Domain

One of the big questions asked about any software request is where does it fit into the bigger picture. This question covers two specific areas. First, the question of where in the application does the Feature fit. Does it need to appear in more than one place? This is called the Application Domain. Second, where does this fit in the Data Domain. Often a software application can have more than one simple data domain to deal with. For example, one domain might be components of a nuclear reactor, while another domain might be inspection schedules. Modeling the Domain, answers these question for everyone and takes the guess work out of it.

Model the Data

The next step in the process is to identify the data that will be manipulated by the Feature. This is typically done in a Data Model. Sometimes, table definitions are imported directly from the production database. Notes are added to indicate changes. If different domains are needed, they are usually placed in different data models. For simplicity and readability, these models are intended to fit on a single page. All data models are contained in a folder called Data Model. When completed, the Data Model folder is linked to the Feature Summary Page.

Model the UI

At this point, the User Interface Model is developed and contained in the folder called User Interface Model. This folder is broken down into two folders. One folder contains models of changes to the existing system. The other folder contains new interfaces to be added to the system.

The User Interface Model makes use of a custom diagram provided by EA that allows the simple prototyping of screens. There is no actual code associated with these prototypes. They are simply symbols that represent controls on a form. Specific details about a form or a report are spelled out in a note.

Once completed, the User Interface Model folder is linked to the Feature Summary Page.

Notes for the Testers

The final piece of the Feature Model actually targets the testing and documentation teams. Acceptance tests that will be needed to validate the software are generated outside the model but from the Use Cases. For each Test Case needed, a diagram is linked to the related Use Cases and placed in the folder called Test Plans. This folder is then linked to the Feature Summary Page.

All sections of the model can be reached by navigating the tree view. But, for convenience, the six main sections are linked to the Feature Summary Page so that anyone viewing the model does not need to jump around in the tree view to find the details they may need. By organizing the Feature Model into a summary page, insures that all the information in the model can be reached easily.

Summary

1. The model is an elaboration of the Feature.

2. User Stories are the highest and simplest expression of a feature.

3. Stories are expanded into requirements.

4. Requirements are organized into Use Cases.

5. The Application and the Data Domains are identified and linked to the Feature Summary.

6. Data Models are created as needed.

7. Mock-ups of the User Interface are created on a custom diagram and linked to the Feature Summary.

8. Notes for the Testers are placed in Test Cases which are linked to associated Use Cases.

Chapter 8: The Use Case Model

The Use Case model contains one folder with the information about the Actors and one folder for each Use Case that is needed. In this example, there is only one Use Case so there will be only two folders in the Use Case Model Folder. As can be seen on the Feature Summary page, the Use Case Model folder shows the folders that are in it.

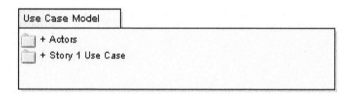

Figure 10 Use Case Model Folder

Clicking on the folder symbol will display the folders inside the Use Case Model.

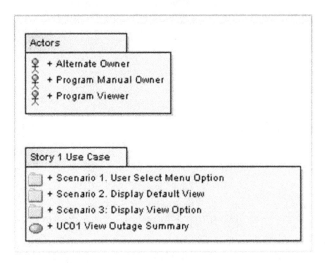

Figure 11 Use Case Model Folders

Clicking on the Actors Folder will display the Actors Diagram. Clicking on the Use Case Folder will display the Use Case Diagram.

The Actors

As can be seen from this view there are three different types of Actors that will be using this feature. All of the Actors will be listed on this folder symbol with a title for each actor. By clicking on the folder symbol, the Actors Diagram is opened showing each Actor on the diagram.

Figure 12 Actors on the Actors Diagram

Clicking on each of the Actors will display the details about the actor.

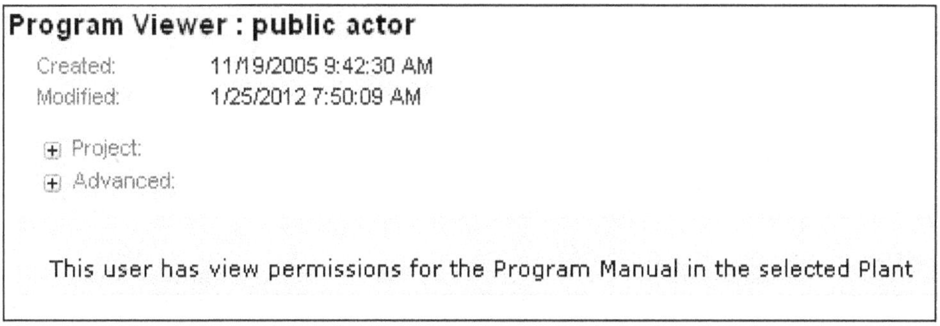

```
Program Viewer : public actor
   Created:        11/19/2005 9:42:30 AM
   Modified:       1/25/2012 7:50:09 AM

   ⊞ Project:
   ⊞ Advanced:


   This user has view permissions for the Program Manual in the selected Plant
```

Figure 13 Actor Description

This is a short and sweet statement about a User. In the context, security profiles have already been established and permissions applied. So, the above statement makes sense to both the client and the development team. No more information than this is really needed. But that is not always the case.

The User is called the Actor because sometimes the one performing the action is not actually a User. Sometimes the Actor is the System itself as in a background process. Sometimes it is a secondary function called from within a function. Most of the time when the Actor is being depicted, the issue being modeled is the permissions that are needed to execute the function. You might say that the UML Actor is role based but that does not have to be the case. Actors in UML diagrams can represent more details than just permissions. When this is the case, the Actor may be referred to as a "Persona."

A Persona is a detailed User profile usually given a proper name like "Sally" or "Sam." The Persona could describe an actual person or an imaginary one that might use the software being requested. Often more than one Persona is developed to help understand who might actually use the software. These Personas can go so far as to imply the experience level of and habits of that particular User. Let's say we have a Persona named Sally. The Persona might read like this:

"Sally is a 32 year old professional who works out three times a week, plays tennis and likes to play World of Warcraft."

At first you may think that this is a very strange way to describe a potential software User but there are several things that can be implied by what has been said if you believe in stereotypes. Knowing this information may give the developer a clue about how to design the User Interface of the request. On the other hand, this knowledge just might give the developer the courage to ask her out. In truth, there is usually more than one type of person that will be using the software. This is where Personas have greater value than the simple UML Actor. The Actor establishes a role or a set of permissions that are needed to execute a function. It does not imply anything about the GUI that might be needed to support the User actually using the software. If the software will be used by more than one type of person, it may be advantageous to flesh out various Personas. This may help the developer decide on GUI options that can give a common ground for the potential Users.

In the Feature Model, Actors or Personas are named in User Stories and referenced in Use Cases. How, the User is identified is something that the development team should agree to and understand the goal of the information implied. Here is a more detailed example of a Persona. This one is from Scott Amblers, the Practice Leader of Agile Development at IBM Corporation.

"Frances Miller

Sixty-seven year-old Frances is the mother of four children and the grandmother of twelve. She lives in her own home, bakes a pie once a week so that she has something to serve for Sunday visitors (usually one of her children and their immediate family), and has two cats. The cats' names are Fred and Wilma, names given to them by four-year old grandson Bobby. She likes to knit and do needlework, which she either gives away as presents to her family or donates to the annual sale to raise money for the church she belongs to.

Every morning she goes for a one hour walk along the lake front when the weather is good. On bad days she'll go with her neighbor to the local mall where a group of senior citizens "Mall Stroll" each morning before sitting down at one of the restaurants for coffee or tea. For breakfast Frances prefers a cup of Earl Grey tea and two slices of whole-wheat toast with her own home-made preserves. Lunch is typically a bowl of soup or a sandwich and then she'll have the opposite for dinner.

She is a middle-class retiree living on a fixed income. Her mortgage has been paid off and she has one credit card which she seldom uses. She has been a customer of the bank for 57 years although has never used an automated teller machine (ATM) and never intends to. She has no patience for phone banking and does not own a computer. Every Monday at 10:30 am she will visit her local bank branch to withdraw enough cash for the week. She prefers to talk with Selma the branch manager or with Robert, a CSR who was a high-school friend of her oldest son." (Amble, 2003-2009)

As you can see, this Persona is quite personal and detailed. The goal here is to understand Frances so that you can make her feel comfortable using the ATM software that will be written. Building a set of Personas would be helpful if you were intending to create a public use web site or, like the example above, software for an ATM machine. When the scope of the software, by its nature, narrows the User diversity, Personas add less value to the project and simple Actors suffice.

The Use Case Diagram

In Figure 6, "The Use Case Model folders", you can see that there is only one Use Case. If there were more Use Cases, each would show as a separate folder. This folder view shows that this Use Case has three Scenarios. Clicking on the folder will cause the Use Case Diagram to be display.

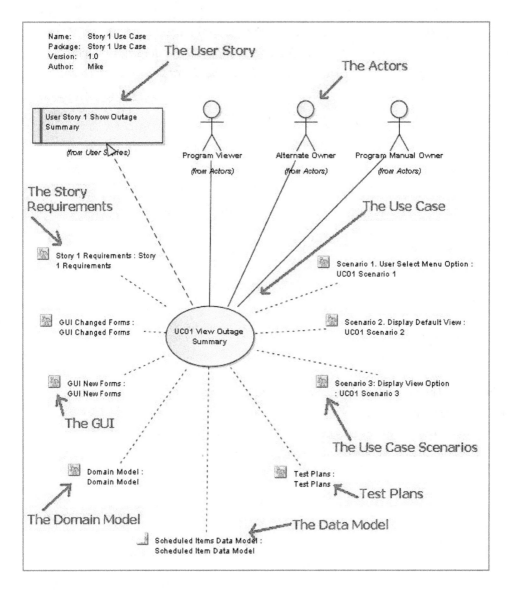

Name: Story 1 Use Case
Package: Story 1 Use Case
Version: 1.0
Author: Mike

The User Story

The Actors

User Story 1 Show Outage Summary

(from User Stories)

Program Viewer

(from Actors)

Alternate Owner

(from Actors)

Program Manual Owner

(from Actors)

The Story Requirements

The Use Case

Story 1 Requirements : Story 1 Requirements

Scenario 1. User Select Menu Option : UC01 Scenario 1

GUI Changed Forms : GUI Changed Forms

UC01 View Outage Summary

Scenario 2. Display Default View : UC01 Scenario 2

GUI New Forms : GUI New Forms

Scenario 3: Display View Option : UC01 Scenario 3

The GUI

The Use Case Scenarios

Domain Model : Domain Model

Test Plans : Test Plans

Test Plans

The Domain Model

The Data Model

Scheduled Items Data Model : Scheduled Item Data Model

Figure 14 Use Case Diagram

Contents and Hyperlinks

The Use Case Diagram is centered on a Use Case. The Use Case is the heart of the Feature Model. All of the necessary information about each Use Case can be found by accessing the links on this diagram.

The diagram should be explored from the top down and from left to right. As you do this, you can see that the User Story that was the source of the Use Case is linked at the top. To the left of the User Story are the Actors that will be using this Use Case. On the middle left you will find the Story Requirements which were generated by the User Story. Below that are links to the Graphical User Interface (GUI) changes and new requirements. At the Center is the Use Case. To the right of the Use Case are the Scenarios that will be performed by the Users of this Use Case. Finally, at the bottom of the diagram is a link to the Data Model that will describe the data to be used by this Use Case. Each of these pieces or models can be accessed from the tree view on the left, but by viewing them from the Use Case Diagram you will be assured that you have seen everything related to the Use Case.

Lines

Lines in the Feature Model are never arbitrary. In the Use Case Diagram, there are three types of lines.

Used By
The solid line is a simple form of association. The meaning of a single line with no arrowhead is determined by the context. When the Use Case is connected to an Actor with a solid line it is read:

Use Case 1 is USED BY Actor 1

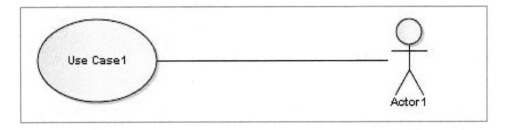

Figure 15 Use Case Diagram – Uses

Realizes

The dotted line with an open triangle arrowhead is a strong relationship. The line is saying that one thing is coming from another. In this case, the Use Case 2 is derived from the User Story 1. This is read:

Use Case 2 REALIZES User Story 1

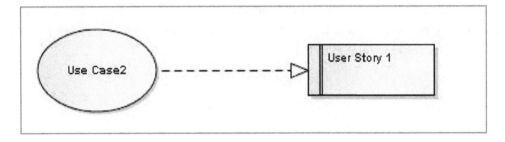

Figure 16 Use Case Diagram - Realizes

Hyperlinks

The third kind of line that is found on the Use Case Diagram is a simple dotted line with no arrowhead. The line connects to a square icon with a diagram. This is not any kind of UML symbol but is a navigation tool provided by Enterprise Architect ®. This line indicates that there is a Hyperlink associated with the object it is connected to which allows you to drill down to another diagram.

Clicking on the Square with the diagram icon will open another diagram.

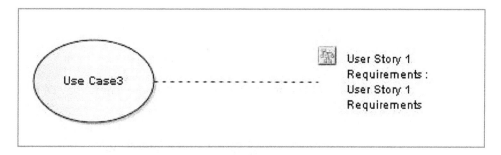

Figure 17 Use Case Diagram – Hyperlink

In this instance, clicking on "User Story1 Requirements" link will open a diagram that has more details about Use Case 3.

Summary

1. The Use Case Diagram is the heart of the Feature Model. There may be one or many Use Case Diagrams in a single Feature Model.

2. Each Use Case Diagram shows an overview of the elaboration of one or more User Stories.

3. The Use Case Diagram is a navigation tool that allows you to "drill" down into all of the details included in the Feature Model about a Use Case.

4. The Use Case Diagram connects the User Story to Actors, Use Cases, Requirements, Data Models and User Interfaces.

5. Lines on the Use Case Diagram indicate Usage by an Actor, Realization of a Story and a link to more diagrams.

6. Clicking on any symbol on the diagram reveals more details about that idea.

7. Clicking on a hyperlink opens another diagram that shows more details about the object it is connected to.

Chapter 9: User Stories

The User Story, or stories that spawned the Use Case can be accessed from the Use Case Diagram by clicking on the symbol labeled User Story.

User Story 1 Show Outage
Summary

The User Story finds it origin in the Extreme Programming or XP methodology and was defined by Brent and Fowler as follows:

"The story is the unit of functionality in an XP project. We demonstrate progress by delivering tested, integrated code that implements a story. A story should be understandable to customers, developer-testable, valuable to the customer, and small enough that the programmers can build half a dozen in an iteration.[13]
(Leffingwell, 2011)

 In the purest use of a User Story it is a single statement placed on a 3x5 card and serves as a reminder to get more details later. Often, the stories are numbered, prioritized and given an estimating value say from 1 to 5 for simple to complex. These estimates are wild guesses or better yet, "a professional feeling" because the story

---

[13] Pg 100 Beck and Fowler quoted by Leffingwell

has almost no details. The Scrum community has adopted the User Story and has defined it as follows:

"A User Story is a brief statement of intent that describes something the system needs to do for the User." (Leffingwell, 2011)[14]

So you might ask, "What is a User Story doing in a Feature Model?" Very simple, "User Stories help bridge the Developer-Customer Communication Gap" (Leffingwell, 2011) and that is exactly the goal of a Feature Model. The User Stories are included in the Feature Model, not as reminders but to spark the logical questions that must arise from a request. The Feature Model attempts to answer the inferred questions. User Stories are simple and easy to understand and help the end User agree to what they want. These stories are also a way to ease the Developer into the model. When the Developer reads the User Story, it will spark questions, but rather than another discussion, hopefully, the answers will be laid out in the model. If the answers cannot be found in the model, a conversation between the modeler and or the stakeholder and the developers will be initiated.

Simply put, User stories are a specifically formatted break down of the User's request. User stories are not a UML standard but combine some key facts about a request. The User Story follows a strict three part formula. The formula is: "So and So, wants something So that...."

Part 1 – the User

Part one of the User Story is the User. The User may be identified as simply "The User." This however has little value. If the User can be more specifically identified in the story then more value is added to the story. For example, the story may open with "The Inspection Supervisor." In this case the title must be understood by all to carry certain system permissions. To "title" a User without a definition of the title has no more value than simply using the word "User." If no titles have been established

---

[14] Pg 100 Mike Cohn quoted by Lefingwell

permissions may be expressed explicitly like, "The User with view permissions" for example.

 A Persona can also be used to open a User Story. From the example above, we could start the User Story by saying "Sally wants.."

Depending on how well you have previously defined "Sally", the use of the name Sally implies the permissions as well as other functions that type of User may be using. Personas are very helpful at the beginning of a project before any User interface (UI) standards have been established. Once a large project has been underway for a while, the UI is established and there are not a lot of choices to make other than permissions. So it may be a good idea to reference Personas when you are first developing an interface but as the system matures, simply referencing an Actor with permissions is enough to get the job done. Keep in mind, the Feature Model is intended to be a bridge between the User and the Developer while not overloading either with extraneous information that is common knowledge.

Part 2 – the Want

The second part of the User Story is the Action the User wishes to take. For example, "Sally wants to view a listing of exams that will be performed monthly." The action can give a hint of the information and the way that it will be presented but it is not specific. The action here can be just about anything. User Stories are not limited to people. The system can be the one wanting an action to be performed. For example a story may be stated like this: "The system must be purged of all records older than 30 days." These stories should be short and to the point. Here are four examples from Ambler (Ambler, 2003-2009) :

1. Students can purchase monthly parking passes online.

2. Parking passes can be paid via credit cards.

3. Parking passes can be paid via PayPal ™.

4. Professors can input student marks.

As you can see, some start with the User, others do not.

Part 3 – the Why

The User Story concludes with the reason the specific function is needed. In Sally's example, we might say, "Sally wants to view a listing of exams that will be performed monthly, so that she can plan how many examiners will be needed." The "so that" part of the User Story does not add directly to the actual request but it gives the "why" a request is needed. The "so that" can imply many things such as an interface to another system, how the data will be used in the future, another new feature or just the personal interests of a particular User that have little or no business value. The point being, that the "so that" part of the User Story identifies the value of the request. You might say the User Story formula reflects the User, the function and the value of the request. The value portion of the User Story is often what is used to determine its priority. Without the "so that", there is no basis for any priority.

In the Feature Model, the User Stories appear as the Feature Symbol with the stereotype of "User Story".

User Stories in the Model

On the User Case Diagram, the related User Story can be seen in the Upper left hand corner.

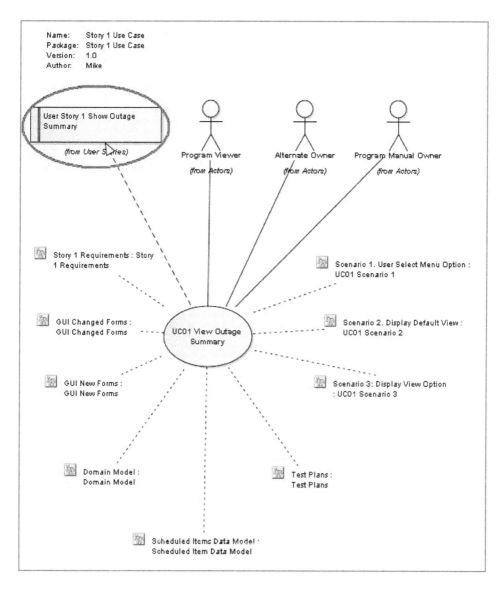

Name: Story 1 Use Case
Package: Story 1 Use Case
Version: 1.0
Author: Mike

User Story 1 Show Outage
Summary

(from User Stories)

Program Viewer

(from Actors)

Alternate Owner

(from Actors)

Program Manual Owner

(from Actors)

Story 1 Requirements : Story
1 Requirements

GUI Changed Forms :
GUI Changed Forms

GUI New Forms :
GUI New Forms

Domain Model :
Domain Model

Scheduled Items Data Model :
Scheduled Item Data Model

UC01 View Outage
Summary

Scenario 1. User Select Menu Option :
UC01 Scenario 1

Scenario 2. Display Default View :
UC01 Scenario 2

Scenario 3: Display View Option
: UC01 Scenario 3

Test Plans :
Test Plans

Clicking on the User Story symbol will display the User Story.

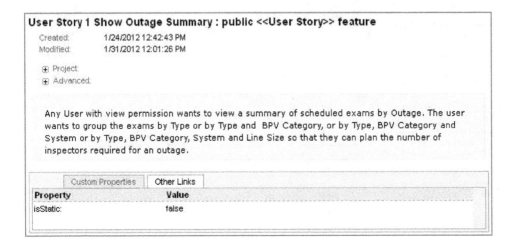

User Story 1 Show Outage Summary : public <<User Story>> feature

Created: 1/24/2012 12:42:43 PM
Modified: 1/31/2012 12:01:26 PM

⊞ Project:
⊞ Advanced:

Any User with view permission wants to view a summary of scheduled exams by Outage. The user wants to group the exams by Type or by Type and BPV Category, or by Type, BPV Category and System or by Type, BPV Category, System and Line Size so that they can plan the number of inspectors required for an outage.

Custom Properties	Other Links
Property	**Value**
isStatic:	false

Figure 18 User Story - 3x5 Card

Think of this panel as a 3x5 card. Each User Story is numbered and has a Title. The story is short and to the point. This story begins with the "Who" in the statement "Any User with view permissions." Since this context has no predefined titles and personas are not being used, all that is expressed here is the level of permission required. It is assumed that those reading the story will understand what "View Permission" means in this context.

The second piece of the story, the "Wants" is stated as "wants to view a summary of scheduled exams by Outage." The concept of a scheduled exam may be new to some reading this story so it is explained in the Glossary section at the root of the model. The "wants" is expanded with more detail by explaining the information that will be shown on this summary. The User Story is not meant to be a specification and must be analyzed by asking more questions later. In the Feature Model, the User Story is basically an introduction to the request at a simple high level. The rest of the model attempts to answer the questions raised by the User Story.

The "why" portion of the story is stated as "So that they can plan the number of inspectors required for an outage." The "so what" portion of the story gives context to the story and sometimes can influence how the feature will be approached.

Summary

1. The User Story originates from the Extreme Programming methodology.

2. The User Story is used in the Feature Model to spark logical questions about a feature.

3. The User Story has a Unique Id and a title.

4. The User Story follows a set pattern: "So and So, wants something So that...."

5. The three parts of a User Story are: Who wants it, What they want and Why they want it.

6. User Stories can be seen by clicking on the User Story Link on the Use Case Diagram.

Chapter 10: User Story Requirements

Obviously, the User Story does not give all the details of a request, nor is it intended to. In a pure Xp environment, the story serves as a reminder to have a conversation with someone about the request so that they can obtain the details when they need them. The User Story Requirements are the result of that conversation. The questions have been asked by the modeler and the answer documented. User Story Requirements answer the first questions raised by a User Story. What is "Required" to implement this story? One way to look at the Requirements in a Feature Model is that they represent the main tasks to complete the request.

In the Feature Model, one or many requirements are tied to a single User Story and are numbered from 1 to whatever within the story. Requirements are a high level set of tasks needed to complete a story. A requirement can be very specific to a system and include details about data or the existing system. A requirement can be used to tell a developer where specific information can be found or what specific information must be shown. For example, a Requirement may be stated as follows: "The system must display Name, Street Address, City and State when the Customer record is selected." The User Story that this Requirement might be tied to would be something like:

 "Sally wants to see Customer information so that she can mail out promotional material."

The first question any developer would have after reading such a story would be "What Customer Information?" The requirement spells out exactly what Customer Information to extract for Sally.

This requirement would be shown as black rectangle with text in the Feature Model.

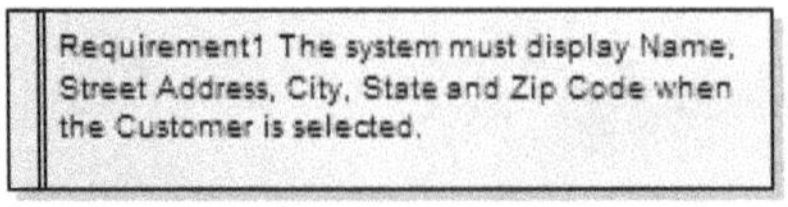

Requirement1 The system must display Name, Street Address, City, State and Zip Code when the Customer is selected.

Figure 19 Requirement

Relationships – which way did they go?

Requirements can be independent statements or they can be related to other requirements. For simplicity, complex requirements can be broken down into multiple requirements in the Feature Model. When this is done, the relationship between the requirements may be indicated by different types of arrows or lines. Arrows do not indicate flow but relationship. Arrows are there to indicate the way a relationship is read. Most relationships can be expressed in terms of "This and That" with the arrow always pointing to the "That" part of the relationship. The type of arrow used indicates the strength of the relationship. There are only five types of relationships that we are concerned with when talking about requirements. They are, (in order of strength); Dependency, Association, Aggregate, Composite and Generalization.

Keep in mind that the "This and That" can be read in any direction. To keep it straight, the "This" in the equation always starts where the arrow begins and the "That" in the equation is always were the arrow ends.

The Dependency

The dependency relationship is stating that one thing uses another. Their relationship is usually short lived. In the human world, you might say a sick person uses a doctor. The dependency relationship is shown as a dotted line with an open arrowhead and is read

THIS USES THAT.

Figure 20 Dependency

In the Feature Model, it is important to note that the thing being used may not be part of the Feature and can exist outside the Feature but is necessary for the creation of the Feature.

The Association

The association is the simplest of relationships. There is no stated dependence or life line indicated in this type of relationship. In fact, they could be labeled THIS and THIS or THAT and THAT. There is no hierarchy in an Association Relationship. You could say that two people are associated. How they are associated is not stated. They could be neighbors, co-workers or fellow church members. The association relationship for a Requirement is simply a single line drawn between them and is read:

THIS IS ASSOCIATED WITH THAT

Figure 21 Association

In an association relationship the two usually exist for the same time and share the same life line. They are independent from one another. The exact nature of this relationship is not shown. The relationship must be determined by the context or it will be stated in the text of the relationship. This type of relationship is more of an informational or design tool rather than a strict object relationship.

There is a second form of an Association relationship that is stronger than the one shown above. This relationship is drawn with a solid line and an open arrowhead and is read:

THIS HAS A THAT

Figure 22 Stronger-has a

This relationship is much like the dependency in that one uses another, but in the association relationship the life lines of the two usually are the same. This relationship does not imply ownership. The thing being used may also be used by other things in the system.

There is a third usage of the Association relationship that indicates navigation from one to the other. The depiction of the relationship is no different than the "has a" relationship and should be noted on the diagram to be clear. The relationship is read:

THIS NAVIGATES TO THAT

Figure 23 Association-navigates to

The Aggregate

The aggregate relationship is a stronger association in that it implies ownership. In an aggregate relationship, the "This" owns "That" and it cannot be owned by anything else. This relationship is drawn with a solid line and an open diamond arrowhead and is read:

THIS OWNS THAT

Figure 24 Aggregate

The Composition

The composition relationship is a very strong. In this relationship, one is actually a part of another. This is used to breakdown a complex idea into smaller parts. The Composition relationship is drawn with a solid line with a filled in arrowhead and is read:

THIS IS PART OF THAT

Figure 25 Composition

The Generalization

A generalization relationship idea is the "That" of the relationship is a general idea where the "This" of the relationship is a specific version of the general idea. The generalization relationship is drawn with a solid line and an open triangle arrowhead and is read:

THIS IS A THAT

Figure 26 Generalization

An example this might be a Dog is an Animal.

Requirements In the Model

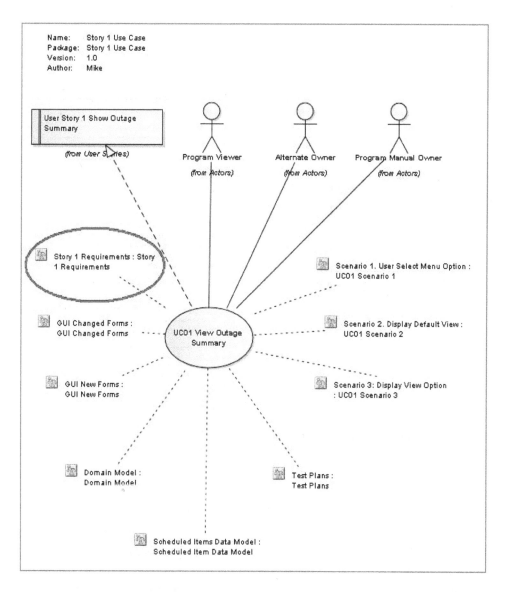

Name: Story 1 Use Case
Package: Story 1 Use Case
Version: 1.0
Author: Mike

User Story 1 Show Outage Summary

(from User Stories)

Program Viewer

(from Actors)

Alternate Owner

(from Actors)

Program Manual Owner

(from Actors)

Story 1 Requirements : Story 1 Requirements

Scenario 1. User Select Menu Option : UC01 Scenario 1

GUI Changed Forms : GUI Changed Forms

UC01 View Outage Summary

Scenario 2. Display Default View : UC01 Scenario 2

GUI New Forms : GUI New Forms

Scenario 3: Display View Option : UC01 Scenario 3

Domain Model : Domain Model

Test Plans : Test Plans

Scheduled Items Data Model : Scheduled Item Data Model

Figure 27 Use Case Diagram - Requirements Selection

Clicking on the Story 1 Requirements Link will open up the Requirements Diagram.

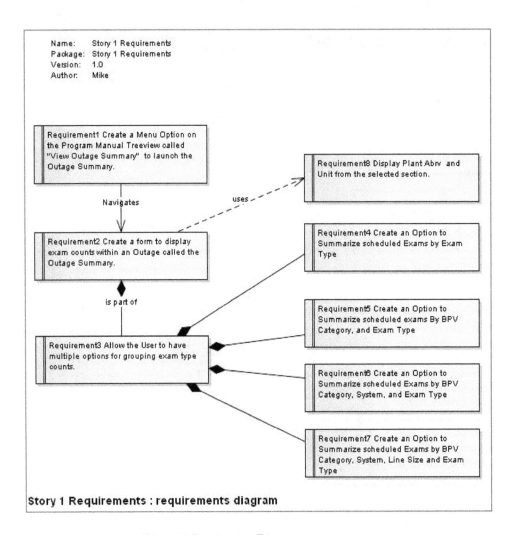

Name: Story 1 Requirements
Package: Story 1 Requirements
Version: 1.0
Author: Mike

Requirement1 Create a Menu Option on the Program Manual Treeview called "View Outage Summary" to launch the Outage Summary.

Requirement8 Display Plant Abrv and Unit from the selected section.

Navigates

uses

Requirement2 Create a form to display exam counts within an Outage called the Outage Summary.

Requirement4 Create an Option to Summarize scheduled Exams by Exam Type

is part of

Requirement5 Create an Option to Summarize scheduled exams By BPV Category, and Exam Type

Requirement3 Allow the User to have multiple options for grouping exam type counts.

Requirement6 Create an Option to Summarize scheduled Exams by BPV Category, System, and Exam Type

Requirement7 Create an Option to Summarize scheduled Exams by BPV Category, System, Line Size and Exam Type

Story 1 Requirements : requirements diagram

Figure 28 Requirements Diagram

From the User Story, a number of questions logically come up. For example; where does the requested feature fit in the scheme of things? How will the User get to the feature? Will there be a Menu Option that will call it or will it be called from another function? In this diagram, there is a requirement labeled Requirement1, to create a menu option to launch the feature. At the heart of the diagram is the actual feature as Requirement2. Requirment3 sets up some specific details for that feature as "part of" the Feature. Requirements 4-7 are modeled as part of Requirement3 showing each of the options as a separate requirement. Finally, Requirement 8 comes from an external source but is used by the Feature. In this case, the Program Manual tree view where the selection was made contains the information needed so the Requirment2 "uses" the information from there.

Requirements Note

Clicking on any of the requirements in this diagram will show the notes that exist on the requirement. Clicking Requirement1, for example, shows some more details about the menu launch as shown in the following figure.

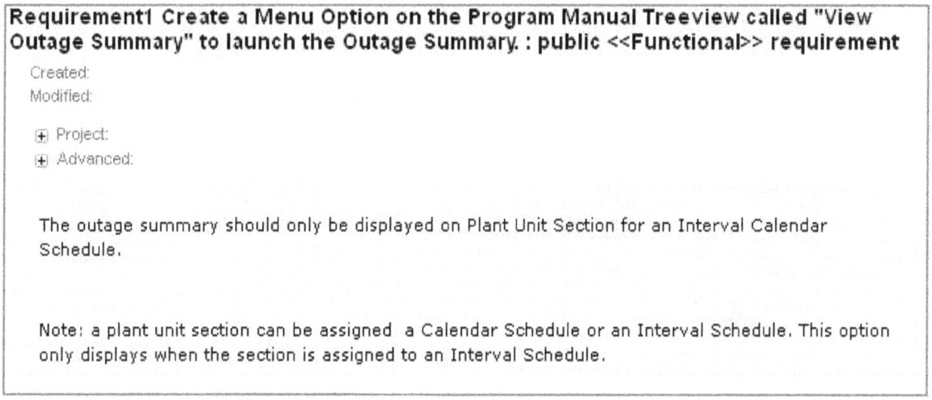

Requirement1 Create a Menu Option on the Program Manual Treeview called "View Outage Summary" to launch the Outage Summary. : public <<Functional>> requirement
Created: Modified: ⊞ Project: ⊞ Advanced: The outage summary should only be displayed on Plant Unit Section for an Interval Calendar Schedule.   Note: a plant unit section can be assigned a Calendar Schedule or an Interval Schedule. This option only displays when the section is assigned to an Interval Schedule.

Figure 29 Requirement Note

Summary

1. Requirements are derived from User Stories.

2. A User Story may have one or many Requirements.

3. Requirements are numbered within the User Story they are associated with.

4. Requirements sometimes exist independently or can be broken down into smaller requirements. When this occurs, the relationship between one another is indicated by UML connectors (i.e. lines and arrowheads).

5. The UML Connectors used on a requirements diagram consist of the Dependency, the Association, the Aggregate, the Composition and the Generalization.

Chapter 11: Use Cases

The simplest definition of a Use Case is a list of steps, typically defining interactions between a role (known in UML as an "Actor" or a System), to achieve a goal. The actor can be a human or an external system.

The Purpose of a Use Case

The purpose of a Use Case is to describe the interaction between the Actor and the Software. Use Cases are uniquely numbered and have a title. In the Feature Model, Use Cases are numbered within the User Story that they are related to. The title of a Use Case is short and usually starts with a verb. The Use Case title starts with a verb because the Use Case describes something that the Actor is doing. The title appears in the center of the Use Case symbol.

The Use Case sits at the center of the diagram and everything is connected to it.

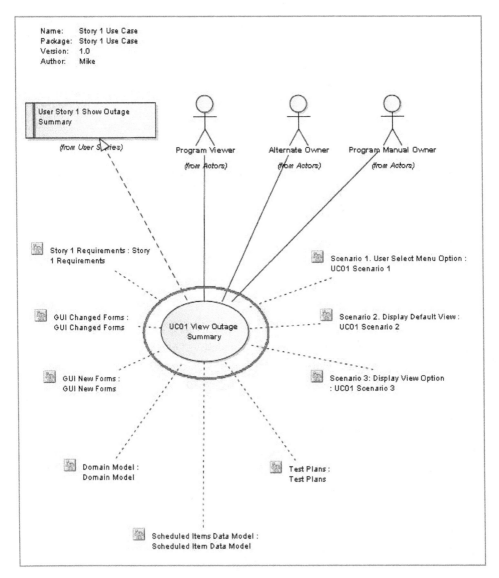

Figure 30 Use Case Diagram - Use Case Selection

The Use Case is the realization of the User Story. All of the User Story details that have been discovered in the modeling process are accessible from this page. Everything on the page can be clicked for more information.

Clicking on the Use Case will display the Use Case Notes.

UC01 View Outage Summary : public usecase
Created:
Modified:

⊞ Project:
⊞ Advanced:

The outage summary is a simple listing of scheduled exam type counts summarized by various user selections.

| Constraints | Scenarios | Other Links |

Constraint	Type	Status
User has permission	Invariant	Approved

⊟ Details:

User has permission to View or is the manual owner or is the manual alternate owner.

| Tree view Popup menu Selected | Invariant | Approved |

⊟ Details:

The user has selected a plant unit section.

| Before an Exam appears, it must be scheduled. | Pre-condition | Approved |

⊟ Details:

Before an Exam appears, it must be scheduled thru the Compliance Plan function.

| The List of Exam Types summarized and shown in a list. | Pre-condition | Approved |

⊟ Details:

Figure 31 Use Case Notes

At the top of the Notes Page is a statement about the Use Case. This statement may be a restatement of the User Story or can contain more background information about the Use Case.

Below the Use Case statement is a set of three tabs. These tabs are the Constraints, the Scenarios and Other Links. The Other Links tab is more or less a housekeeping function of the model and simply keeps a list of links to the Use Case that appear on the Use Case Diagram. It does not provide additional information.

Constraints

Constraints come in various forms and set the stage for the execution of the Use Case. There are three types of constraints used in the Feature Model on the Use Case. They are Invariant, Pre-Condition and Post-Condition.

Invariant Constraint

The invariant constraint is used to describe conditions that must be met outside of the Use Case in order to access it. In the example above, two invariant conditions are identified. The invariant constraints in this example relate to the permissions needed to execute the Use Case. The first states that the User must have "view" permission in the ISI program or the User must be an owner of the Manual to be viewed. The second constraint is that the User will need permission in the specific Plant Unit that will be viewed. A person could have permission to view the ISI Program Manuals but not have permission for all Plant Units. They must have both the general permission to the ISI Program Manual function and the specific permission within a specific Plant Unit.

This information is related to the Actors and more detail could be found by accessing the Actors associated with the Use Case.

Pre-Condition Constraint

The Pre-Condition constraint is used to describe conditions that must be met in order for the Use Case to function. In the example above, the pre-condition stated that in order for data to appear, the exams must be scheduled.

Post-Condition Constraint

The Post-Condition constraint describes the end result of the Use Case. This is a simple case of data being displayed so that is the post-condition of the Use Case. The Post-Condition could very well be the state of new or changed data. In any case, the Post-Condition states what "done" looks like for the Use Case.

Scenarios

The second tab on the Use Case Notes page is called Scenarios.

Figure 32 Use Case Scenarios

Scenarios are the description of the interaction between the Actor and the Use Case functions. Scenarios are numbered within the Use Case and have a Unique Title. Each Scenario is assigned a "type." The type of scenario may be "Basic Path" or "Alternate."

Basic Path

The basic path scenario captures the general flow of a Use Case function. In the example above, there are two basic paths described. This may seem odd at first, but in this Use Case there are two distinct operations. One is the operation of the Menu Option that calls the function. The other is the default behavior of the function itself. These two functions both have basic paths. Therefore, there are two basic paths described here. In a more complex example, the menu operation could be described in a separate Use Case. In this example, each Use Case would have only one Basic Path.

Alternate

The Alternate Path scenario describes the flow of interactions other than the default flow. In the example, there is only one Alternate scenario. This scenario describes the User's selection of options offered by the Use Case.

Scenario Text

The text of each scenario follows a three part formula that I call the 3R's. The 3R formula begins with a Request, then a Response followed by an optional Recovery.

Part 1: The Request

The Request describes the action taken by the Actor. The request usually starts with "The User" but can also simply start with a verb like "Click" or "Highlights."

Part 2: The Response

The Response is the system's response to the request. The idea of a scenario is that it describes blow for blow, what will happen when the User runs this function. So, the Response language is based on what the User sees; not what the system is doing. For example, suppose the User is deleting a record in a list. The User has selected a "Delete" function as the Request. Saying, "The system deletes the record." does not describe the User's experience. To be clear, the response should describe the User's experience. The response for a delete request may read like this. "The system removes the record from the list and issues a message indicating that the record was removed from the database."

Part 3: The Recovery

Murphy lives in software. If it can go wrong, it will. So, the third part of the 3R formula is the recovery when something does not go exactly as planned. In the example, the User is expecting a list to appear. But, the possibility exists that the User may select a Plant Unit or an Outage within that Unit that has no Exams Scheduled. So, a message should be issued to the User so that they know what happened. This is what the Recovery step is for. Not every request made by a User will need a Recovery. It is used only as needed.

The 3R's formula lends itself nicely to being modeled in an Activity Diagram. This has been done in the Feature Model. Links to the Scenario Diagrams can be found on the Use Case Diagrams.

Scenario Diagrams

Each of the Use Case Scenarios are modeled in an activity diagram and linked to the Use Case on the Use Case Diagram with a hyperlink.

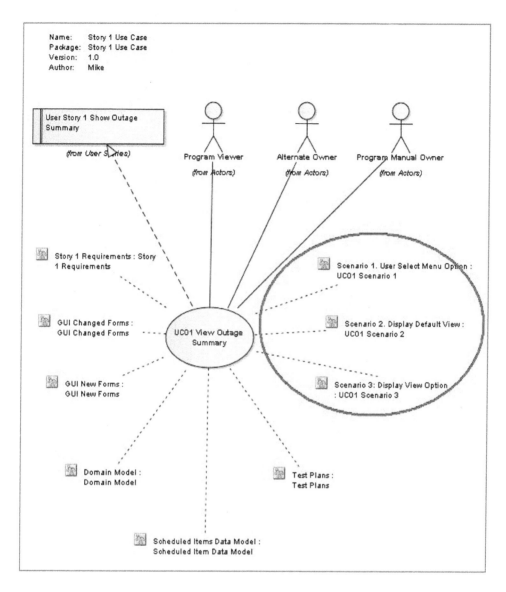

Name: Story 1 Use Case
Package: Story 1 Use Case
Version: 1.0
Author: Mike

User Story 1 Show Outage Summary
(from User Stories)

Program Viewer
(from Actors)

Alternate Owner
(from Actors)

Program Manual Owner
(from Actors)

Story 1 Requirements : Story 1 Requirements

GUI Changed Forms : GUI Changed Forms

GUI New Forms : GUI New Forms

Domain Model : Domain Model

UC01 View Outage Summary

Scenario 1. User Select Menu Option : UC01 Scenario 1

Scenario 2. Display Default View : UC01 Scenario 2

Scenario 3: Display View Option : UC01 Scenario 3

Test Plans : Test Plans

Scheduled Items Data Model : Scheduled Item Data Model

Figure 33 Use Case Diagram - Scenarios

Scenario 1

Clicking on the hyperlink for a Scenario opens the Scenario diagram.

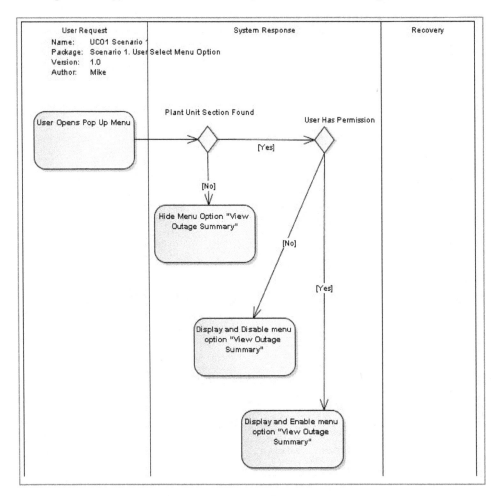

Figure 34 Scenario 1 Diagram

The 3R's formula is applied to the diagram by the use of swim lanes labeled User
Request, System Response and Recovery. The Activities shown in the swim lanes are
executed by the lane heading. The diagram is read from top to bottom and left to
right. Decision points are depicted as diamonds. The decision points are labeled next
to the diamonds with the question being decided at that point. Lines leading away

from the decision points are labeled "Yes" or "No" indicating the decision path for each decision.

Scenario 1 depicts the User interaction with the menu option that will launch the function. The diagram shows that as the User attempts to open the pop-up menu, the system makes two decisions. First, the system decides if the User has launched the menu from a Plant Unit section in the Program Manual. If the answer is "No" the system hides the menu option called "View Outage Summary." Next the System decides if the User has the proper permission to actually execute the function. If the answer is again "No" the system allows the option to be seen, but disables it so that the function cannot be accessed. If, however, both decision results are "Yes" the System shows the menu option "View Outage Summary" and enables it.

As you can see, some very detail business logic is shown by the Scenario Diagram in a very simple fashion. The two unstated business rules here are

1. "Show all menu options that are possible regardless of permission"
2. "Only enable menu options where the User has permission."

As you can see from the diagram, there is no planned "Recovery" for this scenario.

Scenario 2

The second Basic Path of the Use Case is described in Scenario 2. Clicking back to the Use Case Diagram and then Clicking the Scenario 2 hyperlink will show the Scenario 2 Diagram.

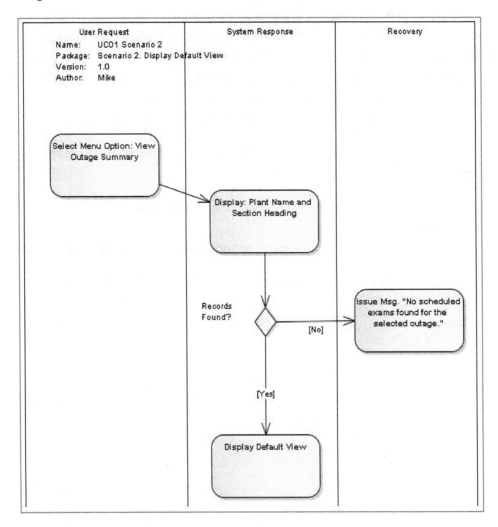

Figure 35 Scenario 2 Diagram

Scenario 2 shows the Basic or "default" behavior of the Use Case for the Outage Summary. In this case, there is a possible condition where a "Recovery" might be necessary. The simple decision point labeled "Records Found?" needs a recovery for the negative response. In this case, the "Recovery" is a simple message to let the User know why no Records were found. This is not a system failure. By design, the User has been allowed to come to this point in the software and to make a decision that results in no data being displayed. This "Recovery" becomes a planned teaching tool for the User to learn what can be done to correct the situation.

Scenario 3

The third scenario in the Use Case is an "Alternate" path. Navigating back to the Use Case Diagram and then clicking the Scenario 3 hyperlink will open the Scenario 3 Diagram.

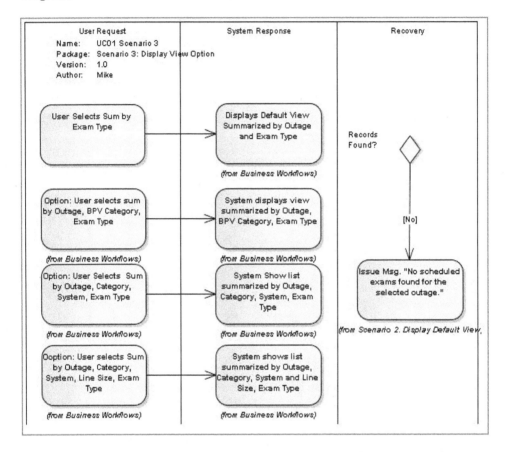

Figure 36 Scenario 3 Diagram

In this diagram a kind of "short hand" has been used. Under a number of the Activities, is the title "(from Business Workflow)." This indicates that the Activity is not original to this diagram. When a title appears under an Activity, it means that the activity was borrowed from another diagram. The title is the general section of the model where the activity came from.

This diagram depicts an Alternate path for the Use Case. In this example, the User may select 3 different options. The behavior is the same as the Base Path but different data is being shown. Not all details are shown. This diagram is assuming that the reader is familiar with the Basic Path of the Use Case before attempting to understand an Alternate.

The Recovery column decision point does not show lines where the question originated. Rather than clutter the diagram with many repeating lines, this short hand indicates that the recovery is the same for all system activities.

Summary

1. Use Cases have Constraints and Scenarios.

2. Constraints come in Three Forms.
    a. The Invariant Constraint describes the conditions **external** to the Use Case to allow it to run.
    b. The Pre-Condition Constraint describes the condition **internal** to the Use Case to allow it to run.
    c. The Post-Condition Constraint describes the condition of the Use Case when it is completed.

3. Scenarios describe the interaction between the Actor and the Software.

4. Scenarios take the form of the 3R's meaning a **Request** is made by the User, followed by a **Response** made by the system and optionally followed by a **Recovery**.

5. The Recovery section of a Scenario is not recovery from a System Error but rather a planned condition that is not the expected result.

6. Scenarios can be written in text or modeled on an Activity Diagram.

Chapter 12: The User Interface

One of the first questions that comes up when a feature is being considered is "What will it look like?" A feature is a small part of a larger system. That means that the basic design of the application's user interface has already been explored and is in use. So the Feature Model does not need to go into detail about color and fonts etc. Instead, the Feature Model only focuses on the most basic aspects of the Form or Report. There are four questions that the Feature Model attempts to answer regarding the User Interface:

1. What data must be displayed on the form or report?
2. What is the basic layout of that data?
3. What existing forms have changed?
4. What new forms are needed?

Enterprise Architect allows the model to create prototypes or mock-ups of forms in a custom diagram. The Feature Model has two hyperlinks that lead to these prototypes. One link points to changes to existing forms. The other points to new forms needed for the Feature.

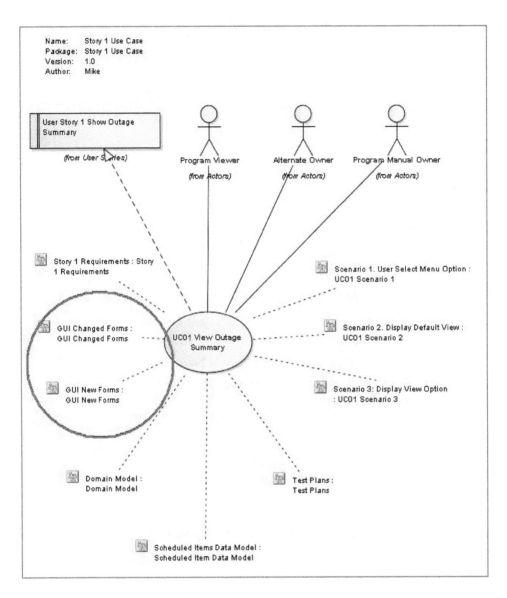

Name: Story 1 Use Case
Package: Story 1 Use Case
Version: 1.0
Author: Mike

User Story 1 Show Outage Summary

(from User Stories)

Program Viewer
(from Actors)

Alternate Owner
(from Actors)

Program Manual Owner
(from Actors)

Story 1 Requirements : Story 1 Requirements

GUI Changed Forms : GUI Changed Forms

GUI New Forms : GUI New Forms

UC01 View Outage Summary

Scenario 1. User Select Menu Option : UC01 Scenario 1

Scenario 2. Display Default View : UC01 Scenario 2

Scenario 3: Display View Option : UC01 Scenario 3

Domain Model : Domain Model

Test Plans : Test Plans

Scheduled Items Data Model : Scheduled Item Data Model

Figure 37 Use Case Diagram-GUI Hyperlinks

Reading the Diagram

The symbols that are used on the diagram are limited and often need text to indicate their meaning. There are some standard symbols that are frequently related to actual controls on a form.

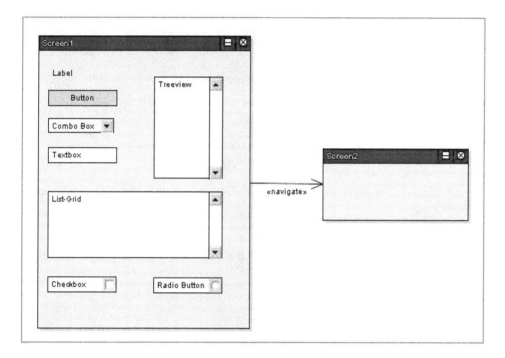

Figure 38 Sample Control Symbols on a Form

In this sample, two forms are shown called Screen1 and Screen2. There is a navigation arrow between the forms that indicates that Screen1 calls Screen2. On Screen1 there are a number of controls depicted.

Here are some of the symbols that can be used in a mock-up.

Label   A label appears as text on the form.

Button   A button appears as a dark gray rectangle with its name in text.

Combo Box ▼   A dropdown combo box appears as an open rectangle with a drop down arrow on the right.

Textbox   A Text Box appears as an open rectangle.

Checkbox ☐   A Check box appears as an open rectangle with an "unchecked" square on the right.

Radio Button ○ A Radio button appears as an open rectangle with an "unchecked" circle on the right.

«navigate»   Navigation between objects is marked by a directional arrow.

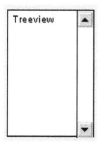

Scrolling containers are shown as an open square or rectangle with a simulated scroll bar on the right. The type of container (i.e. tree view, list, grid) is named on the control.

Although these symbols are very rudimentary, they do a fair job of doing a mockup of a form.

Changed Forms

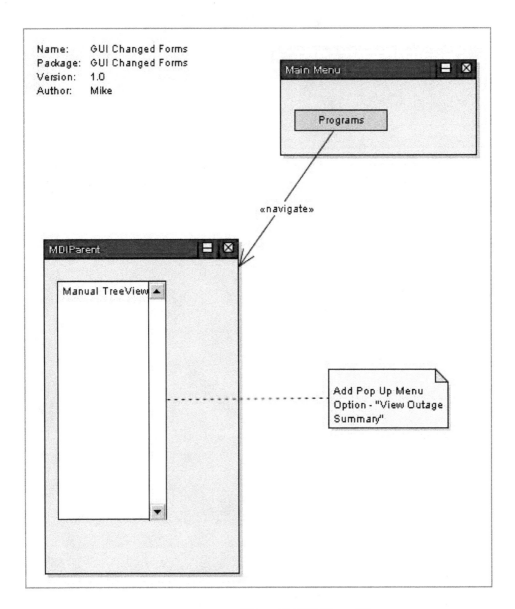

Figure 39 GUI Changed Forms

The Changed Forms diagram depicts mock-ups of forms that already exist in the system. The diagram guides the reader to the form that will be changed by starting at an obvious point. In the above example, the starting point is the main menu of the system. A navigation line points from a button called "Programs" to the form called MDIParent. A single control is shown on the form called "Manual Tree view." A note points to the Manual Tree view control. The note states the change needed to this control.

The intent of this diagram is to guide the reader to a location in the current system that must be changed. This diagram would make little sense if the reader was not familiar the system.

New Forms

New forms are modeled in the same way that the changed forms are modeled. If new forms are needed to accomplish the feature, then a hyperlink to a New Forms diagram will be shown on the Use Case Diagram.

Clicking on the GUI New Forms hyper link will show the New Forms Diagram.

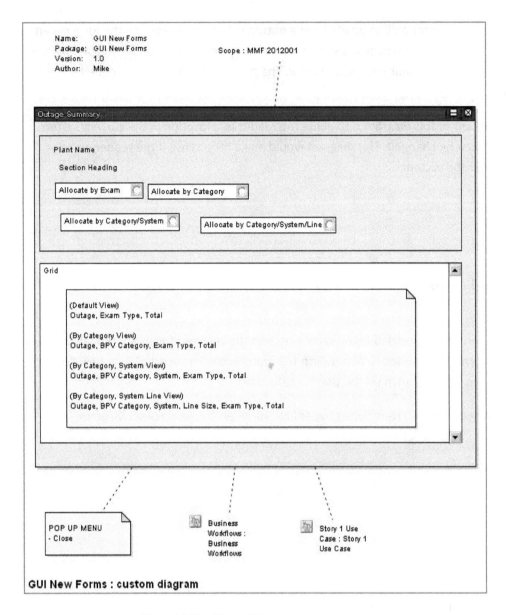

Figure 40 New Forms Diagram

This New Forms diagram shows one new form. The form depicts a panel at the top with a grid in the lower half of the form. A pop-up menu associated with the form is shown as a note attached to the form. This is a view-only form so the only option on this menu is "Close."

The details of what to display in the grid are shown as a note in the center of the grid control. The feature incorporates four different options for viewing the data on this grid. The basics of the layout for each of the options are shown in the note. The "Default View" shows four fields in the grid. The "Category View" shows five fields in the grid. The others follow with the same kind of definition.

There can be more than one form on the New Forms diagram so hyperlinks are added to the diagram to assist the reader in understating which User Story is associated with the form.

Summary

1. The User Interface Diagrams are held in two folders – one for changes, the other for new forms.

2. Either the change or the new forms diagrams can be viewed by clicking on the associated hyperlinks in the Use Case Diagram.

3. The User Interface Diagram contains mockups of forms using facsimiles of various controls.

4. Navigation between objects is indicated by a directional arrow.

5. In some cases, hyperlinks to User Stories or other diagrams may be added to identify which form relates to which requirement.

Chapter 13: The Domain Model

"A Domain Model is a high-level conceptual model, defining physical and abstract objects in an area of interest to the Project. It can be used to document relationships between and responsibilities of conceptual classes (that is, classes that represent the concept of a group of things rather than Classes that define a programming object). It is also useful for defining the terms of a domain." (Sparx)

Sparks calls a domain an "area of interest to the Project." The Feature Model is always about "What to build" but this does lead to two questions that should be answered before coding begins. The first of those two questions is "Where does this feature belong?" Features are not usually standalone pieces of software. They need a home. They are part of a larger system. So, one of the areas of interest to the project would be the main application itself. The question to be answered is "Where in the application does this feature fit". So, the first domain to look at is the "Application Domain".

The second domain is the obvious one. The data. What data will this feature use? Will it change data? Will it move data? So, the second domain, that is an area of interest to the Feature Model, is the Data Domain.

The Domain Model hyperlink is at the bottom left hand side of the Use Case Diagram.

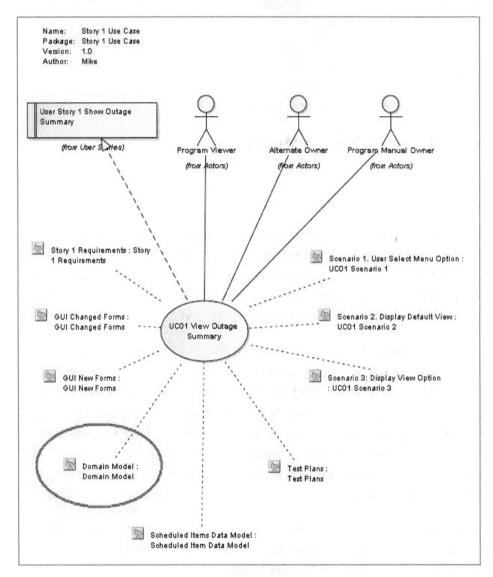

Figure 41 Use Case Diagram - Domain Model Selected

Clicking on the Domain Model hyperlink on the Use Case Diagram will reveal two separate folders.

The two areas of interest are shown in the Domain Model as a folder for the Application Domain and a folder for the Data Domain.

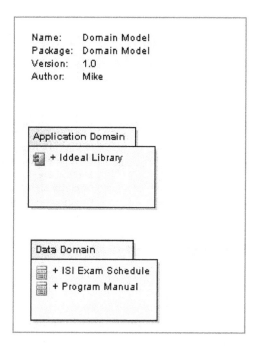

Name: Domain Model
Package: Domain Model
Version: 1.0
Author: Mike

Application Domain
+ Iddeal Library

Data Domain
+ ISI Exam Schedule
+ Program Manual

Figure 42 Domain Model Folders

The Application Domain

The folders represent two domains. First is the Application Domain. In a larger system, the question inevitably comes up. "Where do I put this thing?" The Application Domain diagram attempts to answer that question.

Clicking on the Application Domain Folder opens the Application Domain diagram.

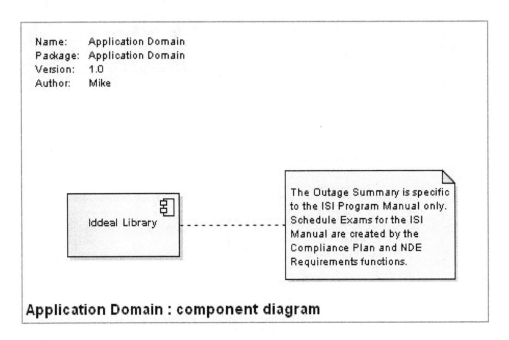

Figure 43 Application Domain Diagram

The Application Domain in this example shows very little new information. In the Feature Statement, is a note that indicates that this Feature is part of the Iddeal Library Module.

The Feature

This Iddeal Software Suite allows the User to view an outage summary from the Plant Unit Section of a Program Manual. This Outage Summary shows the Counts of Scheduled Exams by outage for an interval schedule. The Outage Summary can group the counts by Category, or Category and System, or by Category, System and Line Size.

Affected modules are: the Program Manual section of the Library Module

Affected Programs: ISI

Application Domain

There is a Note on the Domain Diagram that is linked to the ISI Library module. This note gives some specific details about the actual use of the Feature within the Module.

The intent of this diagram is to be a simple reference to show where the Feature will be inserted into the larger application.

The Data Domain

The Data Domain consists of the general area of data that will be affected by or used by the Feature.

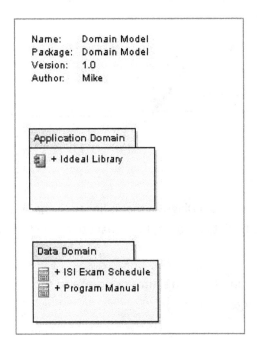

Figure 44 Domain Model

Clicking on the Data Domain folder will display the Data Domain Diagram.

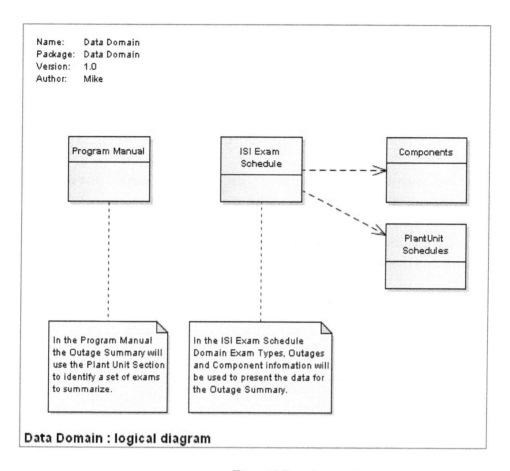

Figure 45 Data Domain Diagram

The Data Domain diagram in this example shows two main domains and two sub domains that are used by the ISI Exam Schedule Domain. The first domain is labeled "Program Manual." As was seen in the Application Domain diagram, the Program Manual is a domain that is maintained by the Iddeal Library Module. The note associated with this Data Domain indicates that there is a specific entity that will be targeted for the Feature. It is called the Plant Unit Section.

The second main domain in this diagram is the ISI Exam Schedule. The diagram shows that the domain also uses two other domains called Components and Plant Unit Schedules. The Note associated with the ISI Exam Schedule Domain indicates the type of data that will come from those domains to support the Feature being constructed.

Summary

1. The Domain Model is a high level view of two separate things.

2. The Domain model contains an Application Domain Diagram that shows the application components that will be affected by the feature.

3. The Domain Model contains a Data Domain Diagram that shows what areas of data that will be affected by or used by the Feature.

4. A note associated with each domain can be used for specific details about a Domain.

Chapter 14: The Data Model

The Most Popular Model

If you have never seen a software model before, but have done any software development, I guarantee that you have seen a Data Model. It is probably the most widely used model of all. It dates back long before UML and software modeling began. It is now, just one of many diagrams that are used by us humans to visualize what goes on in a software system.

There is no one diagram that is essential to the Feature Model. Everything in the Feature Model is intended to bridge the gap between the Customer and the Developer. If something is found in the Feature Model that does not help, then it is waste and should be tossed out. The Data Model is no exception, especially if domains have been adequately established, previously modeled and understood by the development team.

The Data Model is most valuable when introducing new data to the system or the team. The Data Model can show the details of the information that is needed for a new Feature or it can identify data that may have been in the system, but previously not used by the team.

The Data Model Folder can be accessed by clicking on the Data Model hyperlink in the Use Case Diagram.

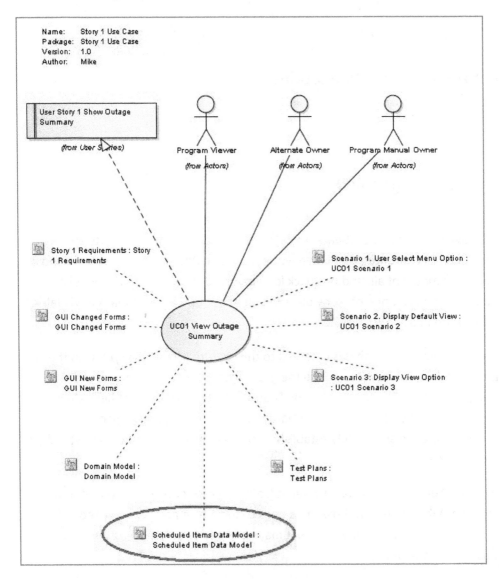

Figure 46 Use Case Diagram- Data Model Selected

The Data Model hyperlink in this example opens the Data Model Diagram because there is only one Data Model Diagram for this feature. In the case where more than one diagram is used, the Data Model hyperlink on the Use Case Diagram would lead to a Model that shows the folders containing the various diagrams. Drilling down on the folders would lead to the Data Model Diagrams.

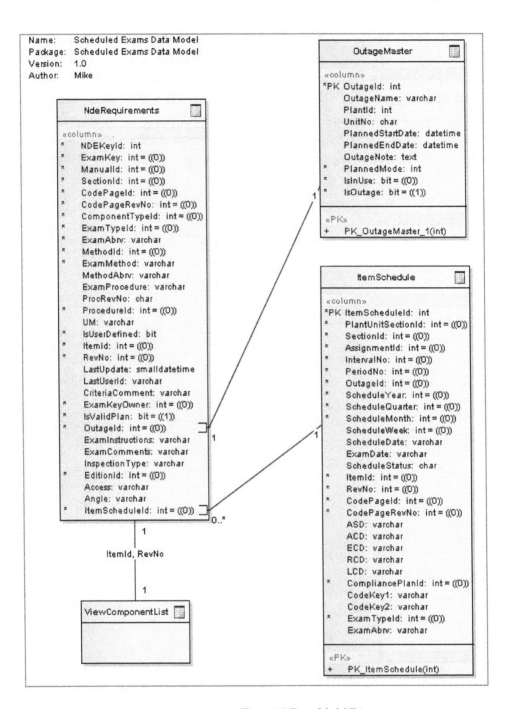

Figure 47 Data Model Diagram

The Data Table

The Data Model in this example contains three tables and a view. The tables show the individual fields that contain the data by name. The data type of each field is shown beside the field name.

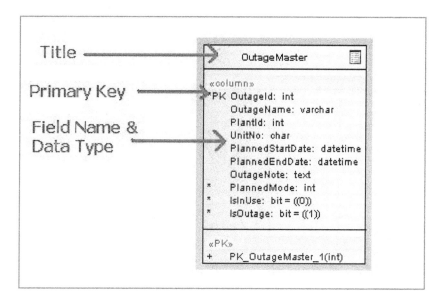

Figure 48 Data Table

The primary key of the table is marked beside the field as PK. In this table the field called "Outageld" is the Primary Key.

Multiplicity Relationships

The Data Model also shows the relationship between the tables with lines and numbers.

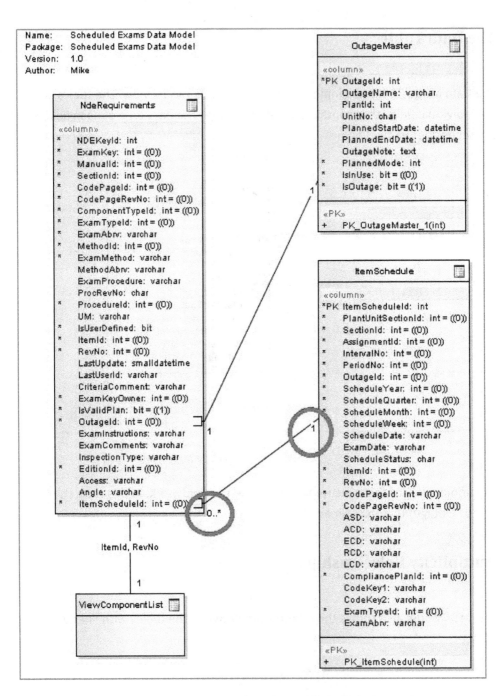

Name: Scheduled Exams Data Model
Package: Scheduled Exams Data Model
Version: 1.0
Author: Mike

OutageMaster

«column»
*PK OutageId: int
    OutageName: varchar
    PlantId: int
    UnitNo: char
    PlannedStartDate: datetime
    PlannedEndDate: datetime
    OutageNote: text
*   PlannedMode: int
*   IsInUse: bit = ((0))
*   IsOutage: bit = ((1))

«PK»
+   PK_OutageMaster_1(int)

NdeRequirements

«column»
*   NDEKeyId: int
*   ExamKey: int = ((0))
*   ManualId: int = ((0))
*   SectionId: int = ((0))
*   CodePageId: int = ((0))
*   CodePageRevNo: int = ((0))
*   ComponentTypeId: int = ((0))
*   ExamTypeId: int = ((0))
*   ExamAbrv: varchar
*   MethodId: int = ((0))
*   ExamMethod: varchar
    MethodAbrv: varchar
    ExamProcedure: varchar
    ProcRevNo: char
*   ProcedureId: int = ((0))
    UM: varchar
*   IsUserDefined: bit
*   ItemId: int = ((0))
*   RevNo: int = ((0))
    LastUpdate: smalldatetime
    LastUserId: varchar
    CriteriaComment: varchar
*   ExamKeyOwner: int = ((0))
*   IsValidPlan: bit = ((1))
*   OutageId: int = ((0))
    ExamInstructions: varchar
    ExamComments: varchar
    InspectionType: varchar
*   EditionId: int = ((0))
    Access: varchar
    Angle: varchar
*   ItemScheduleId: int = ((0))

ItemSchedule

«column»
*PK ItemScheduleId: int
*   PlantUnitSectionId: int = ((0))
*   SectionId: int = ((0))
*   AssignmentId: int = ((0))
*   IntervalNo: int = ((0))
*   PeriodNo: int = ((0))
*   OutageId: int = ((0))
*   ScheduleYear: int = ((0))
*   ScheduleQuarter: int = ((0))
*   ScheduleMonth: int = ((0))
*   ScheduleWeek: int = ((0))
    ScheduleDate: varchar
    ExamDate: varchar
    ScheduleStatus: char
*   ItemId: int = ((0))
*   RevNo: int = ((0))
*   CodePageId: int = ((0))
*   CodePageRevNo: int = ((0))
    ASD: varchar
    ACD: varchar
    ECD: varchar
    RCD: varchar
    LCD: varchar
*   CompliancePlanId: int = ((0))
    CodeKey1: varchar
    CodeKey2: varchar
*   ExamTypeId: int = ((0))
    ExamAbrv: varchar

«PK»
+   PK_ItemSchedule(int)

ItemId, RevNo

ViewComponentList

Figure 49 Data Model - Relationship Symbols

The line between two tables indicates a relationship. The numbers next to the place where the lines connect are called the Cardinality Value. These values express the multiplicity or number of instances that can be expected in a relationship.

The following values can be used on the Data Model

*   Means Many

0   Means None

0..*   Means None to Many

0..1   Means None to One

1   Means One and Only One

1..*   Means One to Many

In the example above, there is a 1 next to the ItemSchedule table on the association line with the NDERequirments table. There is also a 0..* next to the NDERequirmens table. This means that One and Only One Item Schedule Record is expected for Every NDE Requirements Record but no or many NDE Requirements records can be expected for every ItemSchedule Record.

Primary Key Relationships

In this Model, there is one other symbol used at the end of the association line. This is a bracket.

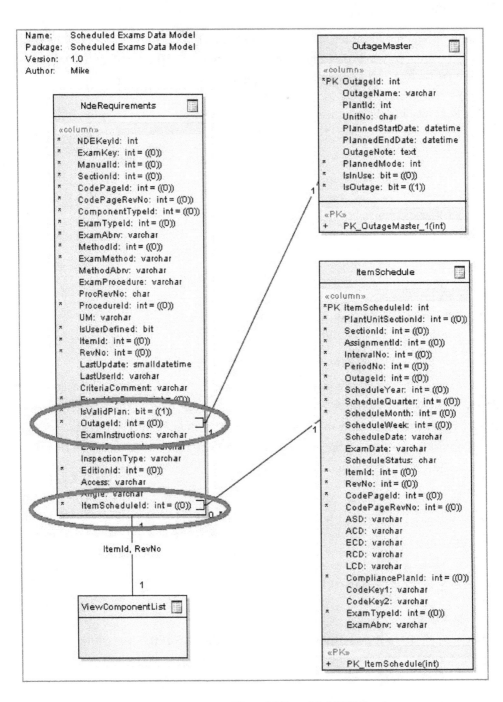

Name: Scheduled Exams Data Model
Package: Scheduled Exams Data Model
Version: 1.0
Author: Mike

OutageMaster

«column»
*PK OutageId: int
     OutageName: varchar
     PlantId: int
     UnitNo: char
     PlannedStartDate: datetime
     PlannedEndDate: datetime
     OutageNote: text
*   PlannedMode: int
*   IsInUse: bit = ((0))
*   IsOutage: bit = ((1))

«PK»
+   PK_OutageMaster_1(int)

NdeRequirements

«column»
*   NDEKeyId: int
*   ExamKey: int = ((0))
*   ManualId: int = ((0))
*   SectionId: int = ((0))
*   CodePageId: int = ((0))
*   CodePageRevNo: int = ((0))
*   ComponentTypeId: int = ((0))
*   ExamTypeId: int = ((0))
*   ExamAbrv: varchar
*   MethodId: int = ((0))
*   ExamMethod: varchar
     MethodAbrv: varchar
     ExamProcedure: varchar
     ProcRevNo: char
*   ProcedureId: int = ((0))
     UM: varchar
*   IsUserDefined: bit
*   ItemId: int = ((0))
*   RevNo: int = ((0))
     LastUpdate: smalldatetime
     LastUserId: varchar
     CriteriaComment: varchar
*   IsValidPlan: bit = ((1))
*   OutageId: int = ((0))
     ExamInstructions: varchar
     InspectionType: varchar
*   EditionId: int = ((0))
     Access: varchar
*   ItemScheduleId: int = ((0))

ItemId, RevNo

ViewComponentList

ItemSchedule

«column»
*PK ItemScheduleId: int
*   PlantUnitSectionId: int = ((0))
*   SectionId: int = ((0))
*   AssignmentId: int = ((0))
*   IntervalNo: int = ((0))
*   PeriodNo: int = ((0))
*   OutageId: int = ((0))
*   ScheduleYear: int = ((0))
*   ScheduleQuarter: int = ((0))
*   ScheduleMonth: int = ((0))
     ScheduleWeek: int = ((0))
     ScheduleDate: varchar
     ExamDate: varchar
     ScheduleStatus: char
*   ItemId: int = ((0))
*   RevNo: int = ((0))
*   CodePageId: int = ((0))
*   CodePageRevNo: int = ((0))
     ASD: varchar
     ACD: varchar
     ECD: varchar
     RCD: varchar
     LCD: varchar
*   CompliancePlanId: int = ((0))
     CodeKey1: varchar
     CodeKey2: varchar
*   ExamTypeId: int = ((0))
     ExamAbrv: varchar

«PK»
+   PK_ItemSchedule(int)

Figure 50 Data Model PK Bracket

The Bracket indicates which field is used in the relationship to link to the Primary Key of the related table. In this example there are two brackets shown in the NDERequirements table. The first bracket indicates that the field called "OutageId" is the foreign key that relates to the primary key in the OutageMaster Table. The second bracket indicates that the field called "ItemScheduleId" is the foreign key that relates to the Primary Key in the ItemSchedule Table.

Non-Primary Key Relationships

When a no-primary-key relationship is used to link two tables, as is the case when using a View in place of a single table, the relationship keys will be noted as the title of the Association.

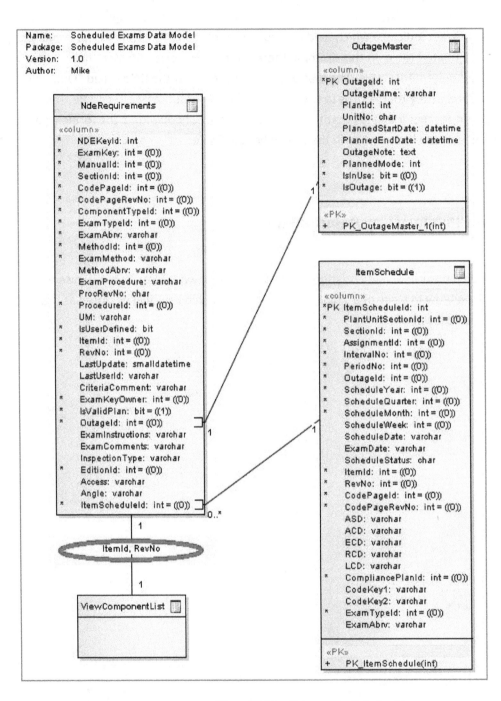

Figure 51 Non-Primary Key Relationship

In the above example, a non-primary-key relationship exists between the NDERequirements table and the ViewComponentList view. The association is shown with a title. The title shows the key fields used as the keys to the relationship.

Summary

1. The Data Model is the oldest and most used diagram in software engineering.

2. The Data Model may or may not be used in a Feature Model depending on how well the Data Domains are understood by the team.

3. The Data Model contains definitions of Data Tables and their relationships to one another.

4. Data relationships involve two components (i.e. Multiplicity and Keys)

5. Numbers and asterisks are used to indicate the Cardinality Value on both sides of a relationship.

6. Foreign Keys to a Primary Key in another table are highlighted with a bracket next to the foreign key field title.

7. Where no Primary Key is involved in the relationship between two tables or views, the key fields used for the relationship are shown in the title of the association.

Chapter 15: Testing the Feature

A Feature is Testable

One of the attributes of a Feature is that it is testable. In order to test a feature, there must be a test plan. The actual test scripts are not included in the Feature Model. The Feature Model is used by the Technical Writer to develop the test plan. To do this, the writer basically follows the Use Case along with its Constraints and Scenarios. As a means of convenience, the Test Plan can be viewed from the Use Case Diagram or from the Feature Model Summary.

Opening the Feature Model Summary node in the tree view and then Clicking on the Feature Model node will open the Feature Model Summary.

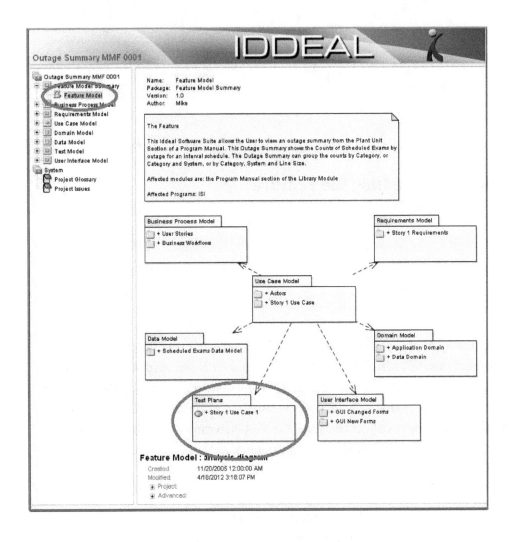

Figure 52 Feature Model Summary - Test Plans Selected

The Test Plans folder is shown at the bottom of the Feature Model Summary. In this example only one plan appears in the Folder.

Clicking on the Test Plans Folder displays the Test Plans Diagram.

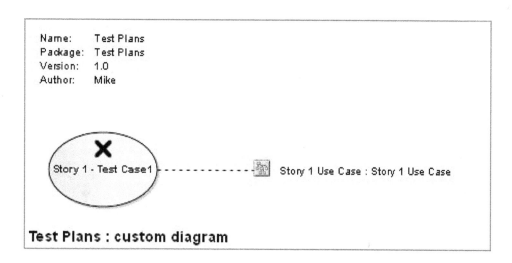

Name: Test Plans
Package: Test Plans
Version: 1.0
Author: Mike

Story 1 - Test Case1 - - - - - - - - - - - - - Story 1 Use Case : Story 1 Use Case

Test Plans : custom diagram

Figure 53 Test Plans Diagram

The Test Plans diagram shows one test Case for each Use Case in the Feature Model. The Test Case symbol is the same as a Use Case symbol but has an X marked at the top.

Test Case Note

Clicking on the Test Case will display the Test Case notes.

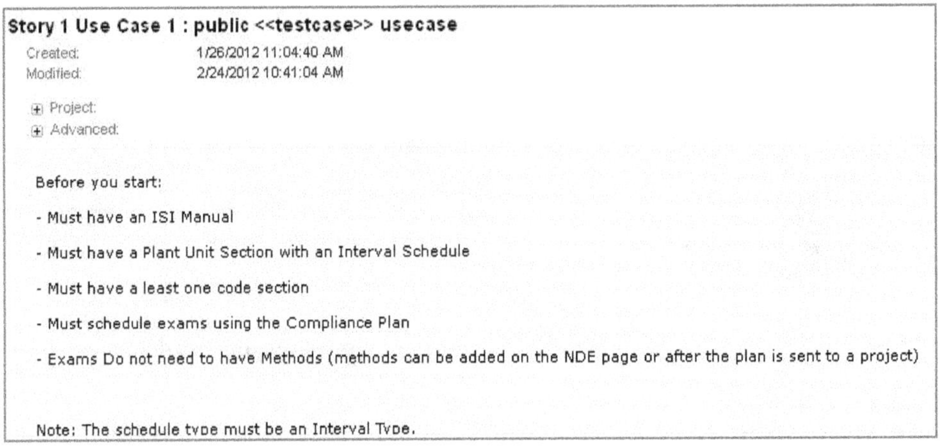

Story 1 Use Case 1 : public <<testcase>> usecase

Created: 1/26/2012 11:04:40 AM
Modified: 2/24/2012 10:41:04 AM

⊞ Project:
⊞ Advanced:

Before you start:

- Must have an ISI Manual

- Must have a Plant Unit Section with an Interval Schedule

- Must have a least one code section

- Must schedule exams using the Compliance Plan

- Exams Do not need to have Methods (methods can be added on the NDE page or after the plan is sent to a project)

Note: The schedule type must be an Interval Type.

Figure 54 Test Plans - Note (part1)

The Test Case note contains background information about the Feature that a tester would need to know. The notes about the Test may be extensive and can be viewed by scrolling down the page.

The first part of this note explains conditions that must be met to prepare for the test.

Scrolling down the page reveals the rest of the note.

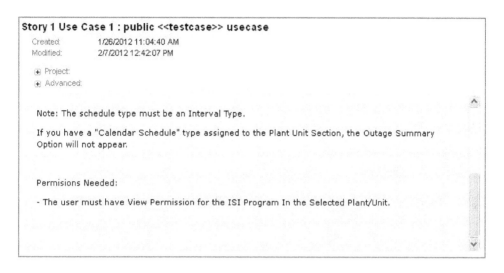

Story 1 Use Case 1 : public <<testcase>> usecase

Created: 1/26/2012 11:04:40 AM
Modified: 2/7/2012 12:42:07 PM

⊞ Project:
⊞ Advanced:

Note: The schedule type must be an Interval Type.

If you have a "Calendar Schedule" type assigned to the Plant Unit Section, the Outage Summary
Option will not appear.

Permisions Needed:

- The user must have View Permission for the ISI Program In the Selected Plant/Unit.

Figure 55 Test Plans - Note (part2)

Part two of the Test Plan Note explains more background information and some
details about the permissions needed to execute the Feature.

Test Case Use Case

Every Test Case is linked to a Use Case. The Use Case describes the interaction
between the User and the System, therefore the Test must verify this interaction.
The Use Case that must be tested may be viewed by clicking the hyperlink connected
to the Test Case. The actual tests are written by the tester to follow the scenarios in
the Use Case. Testing in this way insures that the end result matches the original
intent of the feature.

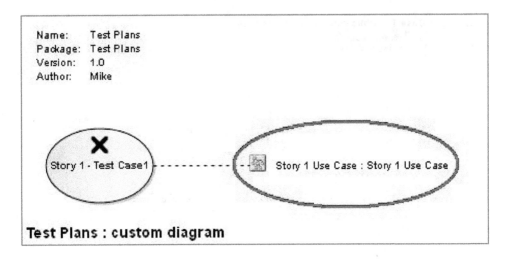

Name: Test Plans
Package: Test Plans
Version: 1.0
Author: Mike

Story 1 - Test Case1 · · · · · · · · · · Story 1 Use Case : Story 1 Use Case

Test Plans : custom diagram

Figure 56 Test Plans - Use Case Hyperlink

The Use Case hyperlink displays the Use Case Diagram.

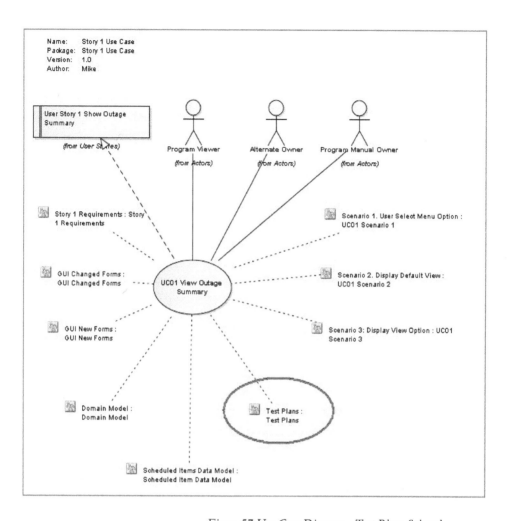

Name: Story 1 Use Case
Package: Story 1 Use Case
Version: 1.0
Author: Mike

User Story 1 Show Outage Summary
(from User States)

Program Viewer (from Actors)
Alternate Owner (from Actors)
Program Manual Owner (from Actors)

Story 1 Requirements : Story 1 Requirements

GUI Changed Forms : GUI Changed Forms

UC01 View Outage Summary

GUI New Forms : GUI New Forms

Domain Model : Domain Model

Scheduled Items Data Model : Scheduled Item Data Model

Scenario 1. User Select Menu Option : UC01 Scenario 1

Scenario 2. Display Default View : UC01 Scenario 2

Scenario 3: Display View Option : UC01 Scenario 3

Test Plans : Test Plans

Figure 57 Use Case Diagram - Test Plans Selected

The Use Case diagram leads to all the information the technical writer needs to develop the Test Scripts for the Feature. For more information refer to the Use Case Diagram section of this manual.

Summary

1. The Test Plan Diagram can be reached from the Feature Summary Diagram or from the Use Case Diagram.

2. The Test Plan in the Feature Model is a guide for the Technical Writer.

3. The Test Plan Diagram shows one Test Case for each Use Case associated with the Feature so that the Test Writer can follow and test each scenario.

4. Test Plans verify the functionality of Use Cases.

5. Each Test Plan has notes that give detailed background about what is needed to create, prepare for and execute a test.

6. Each Test Plan is linked to a Use Case Diagram where the Technical Writer can obtain all necessary information to create the Test Scripts for the Feature.

7. Testing by Use Case Scenario insures that the intent of the Feature is met.

Chapter 16: System Information

At the bottom of the navigation tree view is a section entitled System Information. This section contains two subsections that have information about the Feature called Project Glossary and Project Issues

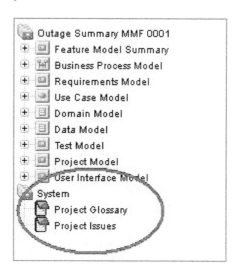

Figure 58 Navigation Tree view - System Section Expanded

Project Glossary

The Project Glossary contains definition of terms used in the Feature Model that may not be familiar to all readers of the Model.

Clicking on the Project Glossary displays the list of terms with the definitions.

Item	Type	Meaning
Calendar Schedule	Business	A Calendar Schedule is used by the IST program. It is made up of many frequencies based on a calendar such as 'Monthly' or Biannually" The Calendar Schedule is setup through the Setup Module. The Calendar Schedule is assigned to a Plant Unit Section at the time the section is created.
Interval Schedule	Business	An Interval Schedule is used by the ISI program. It is usually subdivided into Periods and Outages. The schedule is setup through the Set Module. It is assigned to a Plant Unit Section of the Program Manual when the section is created.
Scheduled Exam	Technical	A scheduled exam is a single record in the NDERequirements Table. It will have an OutageId and an ExamType. It also has a FK to the ItemSchedule Table which identifies what sections in the Manual it belongs to.
Scheduled ISI Exam	Business	A Scheduled Exam is any exam that has been assigned to an Outage. The exam may or may not have

Figure 59 Project Glossary

Project Issues

The Project Issues section contains Issues relating to the Feature that is described in the model. There may be open questions at the time the model was released. The issues will appear here. There may also be ideas that may be incorporated into the feature that have not been reviewed. These also can appear in the Issues Section. Other possible issues might relate to bugs in the system or redesign that is necessary to accomplish the new Feature.

Clicking on the Project Issues node displays the list of issues.

Issue	Date	Owner	Status	Resolver	Date Resolved	Resolution	Notes
Issue1 Should the Outage Summary be allowed against sub sections.	1/26/2012	Mike	Open				This feature allows only the Plant Unit Section to run the Outage Sumary. It may be advantageous to also summarize exams by Std.Code, Aug. and OE code.

Figure 60 Project Issues

Project Issues are numbered. The Issue is stated on the left followed by the Date, the Owner and the Status of the issue at the time of the release of the Feature Model. Notes about the issue are shown on the far right. In this example, an expanded use of the Outage Summary is being presented.

Summary

1. The Feature Model tree view contains a Section called System with two subsections.

2. The two sections at the bottom of the tree view are labeled Project Glossary and Project Issues.

3. The Project Glossary contains key words that may be new to some team members.

4. The Project Issue section contains issues that were discovered during the analysis process. These issues may include problems or bugs in the existing system, possible ideas for the future or just questions left unanswered at the time the model was published.

Chapter 17: Closing the Loop

One Question

The Feature Model is designed to answer one question... What should I build? The model serves several types of individuals. First, the model serves as a tool to verify the Customer's request by giving them a means to visualize their ideas without having to write code. Modeling saves time, money and prevents wasted code. Next, the model becomes the work back log allowing team members to have a basis for estimating the effort and projecting their completions. The Feature Model then becomes a guide for the development team by answering questions about a feature like permissions, flow, look and feel as well as the location of the feature in the greater application and the data that will be used or manipulated by the new feature. Finally, the Feature Model is used by the technical writers to create test scripts that will verify the functionality of each Use Case. This insures that the original intent of the customer is satisfied by the new code.

Feedback Loop

But this is not the end of the Model. This should not be a one way trip. In a Lean environment, there must be constant learning and refinements that trim off the waste. Feedback on the effectiveness of the model is critical. As the model moves from group to group, feedback should be given to the modeler so that the process can be improved.

Lean Goals

The Lean goals of the Feature Model are to reduce wasted time, reduce wasted code, serve the whole team, enhance the picture of the progress and improve quality. Ask the questions. Did the information presented in the model save time, reduce wasted code? If not, what can be changed to make it better on the next feature? Was the model successfully used by the entire team? Was it more effective for some members of the team than others? Ask why. Did the estimates given for the build time pan out? Was there something missing or misleading in the model that could have assisted in a more accurate estimate? And finally, did the model help to improve the quality of the end product?

Trust, Verify, Formalize, Simplify

The Feature Model is a means to an end. It should facilitate both the "Trust but Verify" communication technique and the "Formalize to Simplify" communication technique. It uses standard UML as a formal method of documentation. It is presented by the modeler to the User and the Development team so that they can agree what "done" will look like. Using the Feature model should prevent the classic mistake of setting off in a direction hoping to find a destination. On this trip, everyone knows where they are going.

Bibliography

Amble, S. W. (2003-2009). *Persona*. Retrieved 2012, from Agile Modeling:
   http://www.agilemodeling.com/artifacts/personas.htm

Ambler, S. W. (2003-2009). *Introduction to User Stories*. Retrieved from Agile
   Modeling: http://www.agilemodeling.com/artifacts/userStory.htm

Cockburn, A. (n.d.). *Alister Cockburn*. Retrieved from Why I still use Use Cases.:
   http://alistair.cockburn.us/Why+I+still+use+use+cases

Gilbreth, F. B. (1921). Process Charts, First Steps in Finding the One Best Way to Do
   Work".

Jacobson, Ivar (2012) Succeeding with Agile @ Scale presented at London March 8,
   2012 http://www.ivarjacobson.com/agile_at_scale/

Kennaley, M. (2010). *SDLC 3.0 Beyond a Tacit Understanding of Agile*. Fourth Medium
   Press.

Leffingwell, D. (2011). *Agile Software Requirements, Lean Requirments Practices fo
   rTeams, Programs, and the Enterprise*. Boston, MA: Pearson Education, Inc.

Poppendieck, M. a. (2006). *Implementing Lean Software Development - from Concept
   to Cash*. Addison-Wesley.

Poppendieck.LLC. (n.d.). *Lean Software Development*. Retrieved from
   http://www.poppendieck.com/

Reinertsen, D. (2009). *The Principles of Product Development Flow: Second
   Generation Lean Product Development*.

Royce Dr. Winston W., (1970). Managing the Development of Large Software Systems. http://leadinganswers.typepad.com/leading_answers/files/original_waterfall_paper_winston_royce.pdf

Shalloway, A. a. (2009). *Lean-Agile Pocket Guide for Scrum Teams.* Bellevue, WA: Net Objectives Press.

Sparks, G. (n.d.). Retrieved from www.sparxsystems.com.

Table of Figures

www.ingramcontent.com/pod-product-compliance
Lightning Source LLC
Chambersburg PA
CBHW080418060326
40689CB00019B/4291

* 9 7 8 1 4 7 0 0 4 8 2 9 7 *